HAUNTED
MANSFIELD

HAUNTED
MANSFIELD

Ian Morgan

The History Press

For Brooke – a real-life spirit

First published 2010

The History Press
The Mill, Brimscombe Port
Stroud, Gloucestershire, GL5 2QG
www.thehistorypress.co.uk

British Library Cataloguing in Publication Data.
A catalogue record for this book is available from the British Library.

ISBN 978 0 7524 5530 3
Typesetting and origination by The History Press
Printed in Great Britain
Manufacturing managed by Jellyfish Print Solutions Ltd

Contents

Foreword by Richard Felix		6
Acknowledgements		7
Introduction		9
1.	The Slaying of Bessie Sheppard	11
2.	Harlow Wood and the Ghost that was Cold	16
3.	Mansfield 103.2 and the Ghost of the Airwaves	18
4.	Dame Flogan and the Harte	22
5.	The General and the Sister	26
6.	Sherwood Forest and the Phantom Couple	31
7.	The Restless Spirits of Annesley Hall	35
8.	The Old Forest Glade School	40
9.	King's Mill Hospital and 'Hank the Yank'	44
10.	Lord Byron and the Black Friar	50
11.	The Old Chapel	53
12.	The Ghosts of Bolsover Castle	56
13.	Sookholme, Lukin and the Monks	61
14.	Mill Cottage ...	63
15.	... and the Snooty Fox	65
16.	The Philosopher and Hardwick Old Hall	67
17.	The Carnarvon Arms and the Ship Room	71
18.	The Spectres of Sutton Scarsdale Hall	73
19.	The Fox and Hounds and the Friendly Ghost	77
20.	Rufford Abbey and the Death's Head Monk	81
21.	The Duke and the Quiet Spirit	84
22.	Pleasley Mill and the Wandering Soul	87
23.	A Miscellany of Miner Visitations	92
24.	... and Finally	94
Select Bibliography		95

Foreword

I was delighted when I learned that Ian Morgan had been asked to write a book about haunted Mansfield, and more than honoured when he asked if I would add a word or two in the form of this foreword.

For me, Mansfield is a very special town, as I spent many happy years as a platoon commander in Bath Street Drill Hall, in my Territorial Army Days. As far as I remember there were no ghosts in the building, but I do remember many spirits behind the bar!

I first met Ian when he came to see me in Derby Gaol; I hasten to add that I was not an inmate. It's a tourist attraction from where we run the Derby Ghost Walk. He came to take some photographs of the cells for his new book about Anthony Lingard, who was hanged in front of the gaol and then gibbeted, and by the way still haunts Derby Gaol.

As soon as we met, I realised that we were kindred spirits. His love and enthusiasm of history and its research was only matched by mine. I then realised that he was also into ghosts – 'Hail fellow well met'. We are at present working together on various projects including ghost walks around the UK.

As I was to find out, Ian's knowledge is boundless and his manner of delivering the facts is riveting. I am sure that within the pages of this, Ian's latest book, you will be enthralled with the ghost stories and the history behind them.

I can think of no one better to tell the stories of haunted Mansfield than Ian Morgan, Storyteller Extraordinaire!

Richard Felix, 2010

Acknowledgements

To compile a book such as this takes the good will and help of many people and I am truly indebted to all those named below for their assistance in completing this project. If I should miss out anyone who has made a contribution to this book then please accept my apologies.

My special thanks go to Mr Philip Sanders and Mrs Lilian Rowley for their help with the Old Forest Glade School story. To Andrew Price of the Carnarvon for allowing me to photograph inside the Ship Room and providing access; Dean Griffiths for allowing me into his home at Shirebrook; and to Peter Harrison for recalling his tales of life at Mill Cottage.

My thanks also go to Ian Watkins and John B. Tannen for their time and the complete freedom I was given at Mansfield 103.2, while special mention must also go to Chas Hickling, Brian Meakin, Beryl Perrin, Eve Booker, Jane Stubbings and

Church Street, Mansfield, in the 1950s.

Michael Watkinson of Kings Mill Hospital for their generosity and help in showing me around the hospital. Diane and David Cole of the Fox and Hounds at Blidworth Bottoms deserve recognition for their kindness and for showing me around the pub outside of working hours and for recalling their experiences.

To Christine Paulson I must award a special prize for having the patience to tell me her story more than once, and to John Taylor for adding his own stories to help round-off some of the Hardwick tales.

Liz Weston of Mansfield Museum has provided an invaluable service by allowing me to copy a number of pictures, while Val and Mick Gamble kindly furnished me with photographs of the old Pleasley Mill. Lastly I have to thank the former nurse of Harlow Wood Hospital who, through modesty, has requested to be known simply as E.J.S.

Introduction

What is a ghost? Well, quite frankly I have no idea, and if you were to ask a dozen people the same question you would get a dozen different answers. Have I ever seen a ghost? No, I haven't, and with all the ghost walks I have led over the years you would have thought I would have come across one by now, and yet I know too many sober, down-to-earth people that have had some kind of experience that I am willing to believe that they do exist. So if they do exist, then what is a ghost? There are many theories as to precisely what one is. The general consensus of opinion is that a ghost is the disembodied soul or spirit of a dead person, sometimes these spirits are visible to others and sometimes they are not and it is widely believed that most, if not all, of these spirits do not realise that they are actually dead. Ghosts can make their presence felt in a number of ways, such as being visible to others, making a sound, moving objects, or creating some kind of odour, either a pleasant, fragrant aroma or a more objectionable one.

Theories abound as to how a ghost comes into being. One idea is that these spirits are the souls of long dead people trapped in limbo that are retracing events in their own lives as a kind of self-inflicted punishment. Yet another school of thought espouses that ghosts remain in the land of the living because they enjoyed it so much or are possibly staying behind to take care of the loved ones they left behind. Some of those with a more scientific inclination dismiss all 'ghost' sightings and physical activity as imagination, misinterpretation of natural phenomenon or the visual and material culmination of a scientific process. For those that support the latter idea, it is thought that the ghosts and spirits seen in a particular area are just images from the past that have been recorded in nearby solid structures where the brick or stonework acts as a kind of storage media. The captured scenes are then continually being replayed, and those receptive to these signals are the ones that see these 'ghosts'. That of course does not explain the 'ghosts' seen in the countryside or in parks where structures of brick or stone are nowhere near, or does it? The whole planet is made up of rock and stone so perhaps the images are recorded in that as well?

But what about those times when objects are seen or heard to move? There are many recorded incidents where pieces of furniture, decorative objects or a myriad of other small objects are seen to move or even fly across the room in which the unsuspecting witness was present. This kind of activity is carried out by a ghost commonly called a poltergeist, which comes from the old German words *polte* and *geist* meaning noisy and ghost. On many occasions poltergeist activity takes place in a different area of the building to where our witness is actually residing, but what is the cause of these ghostly actions? Once again there are a number of reasons thrown around, one is that it is a playful spirit performing pranks on those it sees in the area, another is that it is a ghost seeking attention for some unknown reason, and there are those that believe it has nothing to do with ghosts but is in fact a manifestation of the 'victim's' own mental powers. Those that champion this idea say that the human brain has a capacity far beyond that of the simple tasks it performs in everyday use and that the poltergeist activity is simply the brain of the observer using unknown powers to subconsciously make objects move. Who knows?

Whatever you think personally about the subject of ghosts, there have been too many documented events for them to be ignored or dismissed out of hand and perhaps now is the time to open your mind to all possibilities, even to the idea that fear can actually create ghosts.

There is a recorded incident that took place in Hammersmith in 1804 – which at that time was outside London and not yet engulfed into its large sprawling mass – where a pregnant woman saw what she thought was a ghost. For whatever reason, whether through fear or other causes, the woman died two days later. Shortly afterwards, the driver of a carriage was so frightened by the same apparition that he fled in the opposite direction as fast he could, leaving behind his team of horses and all sixteen passengers. The third person known to have seen this spectre was a more hardy soul who, instead of turning and fleeing when he saw this scary sight at a late hour, pulled out his gun and promptly shot it. Sadly for this staunch citizen, he had managed to shoot dead a miller who was returning home from work covered in flour. A tragic demise for an innocent man.

Mansfield and the surrounding area is full of locations and sites that are said to be haunted, so much so that I have had to choose stories which I think will be of most interest to the reader, a task that was not at all easy. The tales you are about to read have been researched from a historical point of view to give credibility to the stories. It is up to you to decide whether or not the reasoning for these events is feasible.

So far no one has successfully proved or disproved the existence of ghosts and perhaps they never will – so do they exist or don't they? It's up to you to decide.

Ian Morgan, 2010

one

The Slaying of Bessie Sheppard

Murder! Discovering a body sounds like a scene from a horror story, but it does happen and it happened in Mansfield in the early part of the nineteenth century.

Every day thousands of motorists travel towards Nottingham on the road from Mansfield that leads past Harlow Wood and towards Ravenshead. At Harlow Wood itself, just as the thickly-wooded area begins to thin out on the left at the bottom of the hill, lies a small marker stone, barely noticeable to the speeding traveller, which tells of a tragic incident that happened on what was then a lonely, unlit country road many years ago.

On 6 July 1817, seventeen-year-old Bessie Sheppard left her home in Papplewick, between Mansfield and Nottingham, to travel to Mansfield in an attempt to find employment, taking with her an umbrella but few other possessions. Perhaps it had been planned for her to stay in the town until she could find work, or it could be that Bessie was just enjoying herself, for she did not return home that day. Whatever the reason for her prolonged stay, it did indeed prove fortunate for her because, after an overnight stay in the town, she was able to procure a job. On the evening of the second day Bessie began her long walk home, travelling up Nottingham Road and past Harlow Wood towards Papplewick. As she approached the bottom of the hill at Harlow Wood, Charles Rotherham, who had been fast asleep on a roadside banking, was disturbed by her passing. On impulse he pulled out a hedge stake from the side of the road and quickly made after Bessie, soon catching her up. Without any warning he hit the poor girl on the left side of the head with all his might, the impact knocking Bessie senseless and sending her spinning to the ground. As she lay on the road, Rotherham then hit her in the face two or three times so hard that her brains protruded from her skull and one eye was knocked out of its socket. Quickly he undid the laces on her clothing in search of hidden money, but found none – Bessie, it seemed, was penniless, so instead he took her umbrella and her shoes to at least gain something for his efforts. Before he left the scene he threw the unfortunate girl's lifeless body into the roadside ditch and then simply walked off in the same direction that both he and Bessie had originally been heading.

Towards the end of the second day Bessie's mother had become concerned about her daughter and the length of time it had taken her to get back from Mansfield, so as the afternoon faded away she gathered herself and set off to see if she could find Bessie. About a mile from Harlow Wood, Mrs Sheppard passed a man going in the other direction, she did not know him but she noticed he was carrying an umbrella. Unbeknown to her she had passed her daughter's killer, Charles Rotherham. Unable to locate her lost daughter, Mrs Sheppard returned home worried, as any parent would be, about the lack of contact from her child.

The following morning some quarrymen were making their way to work when one of them noticed a ha'penny lying on the ground. A quick search of the area brought them to the battered remains of Bessie Sheppard, and nearby they spotted the bloodstained murder weapon – the hedge stake (a later account stated that Bessie's body was first seen by a couple out riding in their gig and it was they who raised the alarm). The police were hurriedly called to the scene in order to try and catch the murderer while a message was sent to the Sheppard household in Papplewick about the tragic demise of Bessie. It is said that Mrs Sheppard took the news of her daughter's death so badly that she went into fits of despair and frenzy. The dead girl's body was taken to Sutton, where a two-day inquest heard all the sordid details.

As the people of the area tried to take in the enormity of the situation, Rotherham had made his way towards Redhill, stopping off at the Ginger Beer House at Seven Mile to try and sell Bessie's shoes. Failing to find a purchaser, he continued his journey until he finally arrived at the Three Crowns Inn at Redhill, where he once again tried to sell the shoes. Still unable to find a buyer, he continued on his journey, leaving the

The spot where Bessie Sheppard was murdered at Harlow Wood.

incriminating shoes behind. Eventually Rotherham made his way to Bunny, where he successfully managed to sell the umbrella, but by now the net was beginning to close in on him. Locals had heard the story of Bessie Sheppard's death and they began to put two and two together and soon the police were called in.

Near to Loughborough, Constable Benjamin Barnes managed to track down and apprehend the killer as he leaned over the side of a bridge looking at the water in the canal below. Offering Constable Barnes no resistance, Rotherham was duly arrested. Yet even then Barnes had to be on his mettle as he managed to keep off an angry crowd that had surrounded them both in an effort to get hold of the killer in an attempt to impose their own justice. The dejected Rotherham admitted his guilt to the constable and told him to let the crowd have him, but the policeman was made of sterner stuff and took his prisoner back to the scene of the crime, where he was quizzed as to his actions. Pointing out the location from where he had torn the hedge stake out of the ground, Rotherham told the constable everything. Popular belief thought that Rotherham had tried to sexually molest the young girl and that he had killed her in an outburst of anger as she fought him off, something that the murderer always denied.

Rotherham was a thirty-three-year-old scissor grinder originally from Sheffield, who was travelling in the area. His eighteen years in the army may have dulled his sense of decency because money was not the apparent motive for the killing; Rotherham had 6s on his person and by his own admission he could not think of any reason why he should have attacked this poor girl. Bessie Sheppard just happened to be in the wrong place at the wrong time. Some of the early reports give Rotherham's first name as William, later changing it to Charles as his trial drew nearer. Regardless of the reason for the murder, and Rotherham's outward remorse, he was put in irons, sent for trial and finally executed on 28 July 1817, just three weeks after the murder was committed.

Rotherham's name soon began to fade from people's memories, yet poor Bessie's did not. Her plight had brought with it a great deal of sympathy and so a collection was made by Anthony Buckles and others to provide a memorial stone so that her name would live on and to ensure that she would not be forgotten.

Soon, however, travellers on the road claimed that as they passed the spot of the memorial stone a strange ghostly figure could be seen nearby. Clearly they thought it was the ghost of Bessie Sheppard. Reports came in from all types of wayfarers, from those out walking, to riders and coachmen, each one insistent about the shadowy figure they had seen. Slowly the sightings became less frequent until, finally, they stopped. The years rolled by and the stone began to weather, while on the road the volume of traffic began to increase. In the 1950s a passing car went out of control, veered off the road and caught the memorial stone, moving it out of position. Not long afterwards a young couple were travelling towards Mansfield after dark when, to their surprise, they saw a ghostly figure floating above Bessie's memorial – angry, perhaps, that her stone had been disturbed.

By the 1960s, it had been decided that the road needed to be widened. Unfortunately, Bessie's stone was in the way, so it was felt that the best course of action was to move it further to one side. As the workmen carried out the necessary road widening the

Charles Rotherham's broadsheet telling the story of his life and execution. (Mansfield Museum)

A full and par-   ticular Account

OF   THE

Life and   Execution of

Charles Rotherham,

Who was Executed at NOTTINGHAM, this Day (Monday), July 28, 1817, for the Wilful Murder of ELIZABETH SHEPHERD, by beating out her brains with a Hedge Stake, on the road between Nottingham and Mansfield.

CHARLES ROTHERHAM, who has this day paid the just forfeit of his life to the offended laws of God and his country, for the cruel, deliberate, horrible, and unprovoked murder of ELIZABETH SHEPHERD, by beating her in so dreadful a manner over the head, and other parts of the body, with a hedge stake, as to cause her death, and then threw her into a ditch, after taking from her an umbrella, and a pair of shoes; he also attempted to take off her gown, but could not accomplish it. The deceased was an interesting girl, about 17 years of age, and daughter of a woman residing at Papplewick; she had left home the preceding day for Mansfield, to enquire after some work, and having succeeded in her mission, was on her return home in the evening alone. Her head presented a most shocking spectacle, being so disfigured that her features could scarcely be recognized; the brains protruded from the skull, and one eye was completely knocked out of the socket, and lay upon her cheek. Some quarry men going to work the next morning, near the spot, observed some halfpence lying on the ground, which induced them to make further search, when, to their astonishment and horror, they perceived the mangled body through the hedge, lying as above described. A gentleman and lady, who happened to be riding by in a gig shortly afterwards, and saw the body, gave information of the circumstance at the Police Office in this town, immediately on their arrival, and the most active steps were immediately taken to trace out and secure the murderer. Immediately after committing the horrid deed, he proceeded to the Three Crowns, Red Hill, where he disposed of the shoes, and sung two songs, that he had previously offered them for sale at the Ginger Beer House, near the 7th mile stone. From Red Hill he was traced on the road to Loughborough, and was taken on the bridge leading over the canal near to that place. He was looking over the bridge into the water, when the constable approached him, and accosted him with being his prisoner; he made no resistance.

When he was taken to be present at the inquest, he did not hesitate to show the constable the spot where the murder was committed. The hedge stake was found within a few yards of the place, besmeared with blood. The body was removed to Sutton, where a Coroner's inquest sat for two days.

It would appear that the unhappy mother was fated to meet the ruthless murderer of her hapless child on the public highway, soon after the horrid deed had been committed, and not more than a mile from the place. Feeling an anxious desire for her daughter's return, she went out towards the evening to meet her, when the murderer passed her on the way, with an umbrella under his arm, the same he had taken away from the unfortunate female. Ever since the mother heard the news of this horrid transaction, her mind has continued in a state of phrenzy.

A Friend, who visited him in prison, asked him, what could induce him to commit so horrid an act? he replied, "I know not; I had laid down under a bank and slept, and when I awoke, the unfortunate girl happened to be passing by, and a hedge stake being at hand, I instantly took it up, and with one blow did the business; I then took the shoes and umbrella, and proceeded to Red Hill, where I slept soundly all the night. I am indifferent what they do with my body, as I deserve the worst punishment they can inflict. The poor victim of my barbarity had not a moment to repent; I have had time to prepare, and hope I have made good use of it."

He never attempted to deny his guilt, but, on the contrary, always declared it, and considered his sentence the just reward of his abominable crime, and bowed submissive to the mandate of his earthly judge. From the time of his commitment to that of his execution, he has behaved with great penitence, employing nearly the whole of his time to reading the Testament; he has received the friendly assistance of the Rev. Mr. Bryan, and others, who were assiduous in their exertions to prepare him for the awful moment, when he must appear at the unerring tribunal of the Almighty Judge, from whom he expressed his full hope of receiving pardon and forgiveness for his enormous crimes. He was 33 years of age, of very small stature, of a melancholy countenance, a native of Sheffield, by trade a scissor-grinder, and had served upwards of 18 years in the army. He has left a wife to lament his untimely end.

He was brought forth from the prison, at seven o'clock, and conveyed in a cart to the place of execution, amidst an immense concourse of spectators; he appeared perfectly resigned to his unhappy fate, and after a short time spent in prayer, he was launched into eternity, other hanging the usual time, his body was delivered to the surgeons for dissection.

[S. BARBER, Printer, Chamber Street, Nottingham.

Bessie Sheppard's stone.

memorial stone was removed, a new inscription placed upon it and finally it was replaced in its new position. Since then there have been many sightings and reports of an unusual figure in the area of the stone, with some of the witnesses claiming to have seen a young woman carrying an umbrella and looking distressed. Others say that the figure appears to be lost and on occasions drivers have even stopped to offer the woman a lift, only to see her vanish before their eyes. Perhaps Bessie Sheppard is unhappy that her stone is not where it should be, or perhaps she is keen to ensure that her plight should not be forgotten.

two

Harlow Wood and the Ghost that was Cold

When Harlow Wood Hospital opened in 1929, it had the prospect of a long and successful lifespan: set a little way out of Mansfield and surrounded by woodlands it offered the latest in cutting edge medical treatment. As the years rolled by the staff learned the tried and tested methods of healing the sick and frequently drew on their own knowledge to get them through. By the late 1970s many of the doctors and nurses had decades of know-how behind them with one nurse, simply known as E.J.S., able to draw on over thirty year's experience. It was while on night duty that she encountered a situation that no amount of training could have prepared her for and calm reasoning was to have no effect.

As the hospital ward was settling down for the night, it was E.J.S.'s duty to make sure that everything was in its rightful place and that all vital equipment was in good order. Sometime between 10 and 10.30 p.m., E.J.S. and an auxiliary nurse walked down the ward to check out the fire doors. As they made their way down they passed a number of side wards, some with six beds, some with less. Most of the lights were off with only a small light over the nurses' station and just dim lighting in the corridor giving any form of illumination. Nearly all of the patients were asleep and the ward had settled after a long day. At the end of the ward the two nurses made a final check on the fire doors and oxygen bottles, satisfying themselves that the ward could be 'shut down' for the night. Walking back towards the nurses' station, they were suddenly taken aback by the sound of a child's voice saying, 'I'm so cold'. The two nurses looked at each other in disbelief; there were no children on the ward and yet both E.J.S. and her colleague had clearly heard the voice.

Shaken, both nurses continued to make their way back to the top of the ward, but as they passed the open door of a single-bedded side ward, the male patient inside enquired if there was a child nearby. Naturally he was given the answer that there was not and yet he insisted that he had clearly heard a child's voice speak, and he repeated those words, 'I'm so cold', adding that he thought it was a nice voice. In order to reassure the patient and to save any distress, both nurses played down the situation by claiming they had heard nothing. So terrified were E.J.S. and the auxiliary that they clung to each other as they made their way back to their station. Once there they rang the night sister and told her of their experience. Within minutes the sister had joined the nurses on the ward and, to calm their nerves, she sat them down with a cup of tea.

The child never did come back, well not to E.J.S. and her colleague any way, and no one else spoke of coming across this cold youngster, but you have to ask yourself, was it Bessie Sheppard, who died just yards away? (*See* Chapter One) After all, a number of the staff had reported seeing a lonely figure standing in the woods close to the scene of Bessie's murder.

By the mid-1990s the decision had been taken to close Harlow Wood Hospital and to sell off the land for housing, so in 1995 the doors closed for the last time and any chance of finding out who the lost child was had gone. The workmen soon moved in and began to demolish the buildings, making way for new houses to be built. Near the entrance to the site stood an old house, its vacant rooms and empty windows giving a creepy look to the place as it lay in the shadows of the trees. Soon the security men who were looking after the building site began to protest that they kept seeing the eerie figure of a nurse looking out of a bedroom window. Even more alarming for them was that the window appeared to be lit by candlelight. No proof was ever found that there had been someone in the house but the guards were so anxious about the ethereal shape they would not patrol that part of the site. In the end the construction company decided to board up the upstairs windows in an attempt to alleviate the situation.

The last word must rest with a patient of one of the hospital wards, someone who was sad to see the old place go. When the keys turned in the lock of Ward 6 for the last time a voice from inside the now vacant ward was distinctly heard to say 'Goodbye'.

Harlow Wood, where a lonely figure has been seen standing close to the scene of Bessie Sheppard's murder.

three

Mansfield 103.2 and the Ghost of the Airwaves

If a policeman were to stop you in the street and ask where you were at eight o'clock on the morning of Monday, 28 July 2008, you probably would not have any idea. And yet for many people the events of that morning were something that they would remember for a long time. What had taken place on that day? Weston-Super-Mare's famous Grand Pier had suffered a disastrous fire for the second time in eighty years – bringing it to the attention of the world's press. Yet something much closer to home had made a large number of people stop and listen. Could it be a hoax or had they really heard an unearthly voice coming over the airwaves and out of their radio?

At Radio Mansfield 103.2 that Monday morning John B. Tannen had been busily working away in studio one at the radio station on Samuel Brunts Way, playing tracks that would hopefully bring some cheer to the listeners as they started their working week. As the clock moved toward the hour, he knew it would soon be time for Ian Watkins to take to the airwaves and read the eight o'clock news. Just before 8 a.m. Ian entered the studio and asked those inside to leave for a short while so that his broadcast could be made; a quite normal procedure to ensure no distractions or background noise. Standing behind the control console he had command of all the buttons and switches that he would need to make the news announcements, while in front of the console he could see into studio two through a clear glass window. Now alone in the studio, Ian waited for the final seconds to pass as the clock rapidly reached the hour. Outside the door in the corridor stood John, waiting for his cue to re-enter and continue his programme when the news had been read. Each of the studios is designed so that external noise cannot penetrate and disrupt the broadcast and even the windows are designed specifically to keep outside sounds to a minimum, including the large plate-glass window that allows you to look into studio one from the corridor.

With his news bulletin just seconds away and the news announcement jingle playing, Ian opened the microphone to speak but as the jingle died away to silence he was left speechless when, through his headphones, the quiet was broken by a voice clearly saying '...time.' This unexpected voice threw his concentration and for a few seconds Ian was unable to start his broadcast. Outside the door John also heard the voice coming over an external speaker and momentarily thought he was being prompted to return to continue his show, until he realised the news bulletin had not even started. After successfully composing himself and completing the news, Ian left the room to allow his colleague to return and carry on with his programme. Safely out of the studio, he asked the soundman if he had also heard the voice, which he confirmed he had done. So had the listeners to the station, and a number of people rang in to question what they had heard? The programme log tapes, which have to be kept for nine weeks, were checked to see if the unexpected voice had been recorded and there it was, clear for all to hear. Could it have been a voice coming over the station's tannoy system and accidentally being picked up in the studio? A quick question to John soon discounted that idea because, while in the corridor, he could clearly see the tannoy buttons and nobody had used it. Was it interference from inside studio one itself? Could the minidisk player to the right of and behind the console been accidentally activated and the contents of a disc broadcast? No – the fader for the disc was off and there was no disc in the player. Could a problem next door in studio two have caused the sound? But this too was quickly ruled out.

John B. Tannen and Ian Watkins (right) in studio one at Radio Mansfield 103.2.

To discount any fault in the machinery, Ian decided to perform the nine o'clock news using exactly the same routine as before; this time nothing untoward happened. The source of the voice remained a mystery but this was not the first time strange things had happened in that studio. Occasionally the door to the studio will open by itself, even though it has an automatic closer fitted. Elsewhere in the building, in one of the corridors, the smell of tobacco sometimes pervades the air, despite the building having a no-smoking policy, while in other parts the staff can be left with the sensation that they are not alone. The late night newsreader frequently hears the sound of falling objects coming from the empty offices upstairs. In the news room items are knocked over by an unseen entity that, up to now, seems to bear no malice toward the living.

The story of the ghostly voice could easily be discounted as a prank or hoax to stimulate the listeners, however, something took place some time before that was kept from the listening public.

Very often items that are to be broadcast as part of the news bulletin are pre-recorded so that, if necessary, they can be edited to ensure that they fit into the limited time allowed for the announcements. One of these articles was being recorded by James Corden so that it could later be tailored to a more suitable length to fit into the bulletin. This particular news item was a telephone interview with a lady regarding a topical subject of the day. As the conversation progressed and with the recording machine capturing everything, James asked the lady a question to which she easily responded, yet, as she spoke, there was clearly heard a voice saying 'liar'. Without pausing, the lady

The building where Mansfield 103.2 is broadcast, with studio one overlooking the grass.

Brunts School in its early years. (Mansfield Museum)

continued her answer and it was clear that she had either ignored the voice or had not heard it at all. With the interview concluded, James played the tape back and there, plain to hear, was the unearthly voice. Others listened to the tape and agreed that this was definitely something that should not be broadcast lest it be misconstrued as an opinion to the lady's comments. To make sure in their own minds that the voice was genuine, all the equipment was checked and all outside possibilities for interference were verified as impossible, and just like the happenings that later took place in studio one, nothing was found which could explain the voice.

The building that Mansfield 103.2 occupies was constructed in the early 1890s as part of the now long gone Brunts Technical School, just off Woodhouse Road, near to the town centre. In 1709 Samuel Brunts left a bequest to provide for local children to learn a trade that would be honest and see them do well in life, and it was this generosity and the increase in the value of his bequest that led to the new school bearing his name. Perhaps Brunts, one of the former masters at the school, or one of the old pupils is playing a series of jokes on the staff at the radio station? Of course it could be someone from an even older time because the school was built on land near the heart of the town and there is every likelihood that another building could have been on the site many years ago. It would be nice to think that whoever it is is marvelling at the wonders of modern technology and enjoying listening to the music.

four

Dame Flogan and the Harte

Running through the heart of Mansfield is a huge railway viaduct, its arches framing the town centre as if it were being seen through some giant shop window. To one side of the arches lie a whole row of buildings that front onto the market place while on the other side is White Hart Street, a shopping area that houses some of the older shops in the town, running down the side away from the arches. A short way down this well used thoroughfare lies Dame Flogan Street, a short road used by motorists and pedestrians alike as a shortcut through to Midworth Street and then to the ring road. The odd thing is that although most of those using this shortcut know the name of the street, the vast majority have no idea who Dame Flogan was or what she did to achieve the honour of having a street named after her.

Dame Cicely Flogan was one of those people in history that mixed with the rich and noble families of the day and was able to take advantage of such high ranking companions. In her will of 1521 she left a large amount of land and property that was to be used to maintain a priest to say Mass and to sing in Mansfield's parish church (or the Chapel of St Lawrence) for the souls of herself and her relatives. This same priest was to fulfil a whole host of other religious duties in compliance of Dame Flogan's wishes, which included this good man of the cloth receiving payment for his services. The church bells were also to be rung on each anniversary of her death, for which the clerk of the church was to receive 4*d*.

Dame Flogan's final request was to be short-lived when, in 1548, a survey was made of all the chantrys and, along with all those of a similar nature, all properties and goods were seized. With her original bequest ended, the monies were directed to benefit the Church, and indirectly to help the poor, and later to educate those at the Grammar School. Directly or indirectly, this wealthy woman has helped the people of Mansfield for nearly 500 years. Yet for all her wealth, Dame Flogan suffered a tragic death when, as legend has it, she was dragged a short distance by a horse before dying from the injuries she received. Perhaps more poignantly she died near her home and within sight of the parish church she loved so much.

Her house was undoubtedly one of the more opulent ones in the area, with the lower part constructed from stone while the upper floor was a mixture of timber, stone and plaster, and atop this the roof was made of stone slabs. Her home bore the name 'Harte' and since its demolition the 'White Hart' pub has stood on its site. Could it be Dame Flogan that is seen walking the streets near to the pub? Her ghost is said

Church Street, Mansfield, c. 1910. (Mansfield Museum)

to haunt White Hart Street and Dame Flogan Street, so if you should see a shadowy figure in either of these places then you know who it is.

Nor does the White Hart itself escape her attentions, as many sightings of unexplained visitors have been recorded, and yet possibly she is not alone in her wanderings as the descriptions of those spirits vary a great deal.

One of the upstairs rooms in this three-storey building is constantly cold regardless of how high the heating is turned up, to the point that one landlord used to keep perishable foods in there so that they would keep longer. While this particular inn keeper took advantage of the situation, others have had a number of problems when trying to go about their everyday duties. One unfortunate landlord decided to retrieve the pub keys from their usual spot behind the bar only to discover that they had gone. For twenty-five minutes he and other members of the staff searched for the missing keys only to find that they had been put back in their normal place. That was the last time that they were hung in that location. This same landlord's dog used to stand at the bottom of the stairs that work their way down into the bar area and bark vigorously at some unseen entity. On other occasions a misty shape has been seen coming down those same stairs and entering the customer area of the pub. Whether it is a man or woman is open to speculation, for after hundreds of years of human habitation on this site it could be anyone who lived or died there. Dame Flogan is the obvious choice,

The White Hart, Mansfield.

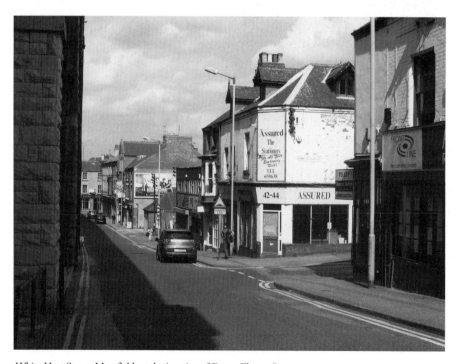

White Hart Street, Mansfield, at the junction of Dame Flogan Street.

The old White Hart Inn, by A.S. Buxton (1867-1932). (Mansfield Museum)

after all it was her house that stood on the site for many years, but this does not explain the spectral figure of a man seen in the bar.

While the landlord and his wife were preparing for the day ahead, the landlady noticed a man sat at the corner of the bar facing towards her and her husband and with his back to the outside door of the inn. With the pub still closed to the public and the entrance door locked, she was taken aback to see someone inside and obviously wanting to ply his custom. Quickly she pointed out the 'customer' to her husband, who turned to look at the stranger. Unable to comprehend how the man had got into the pub, he turned back to speak to his wife but when he took a second look at the man he found that the visitor had vanished. Where he had gone remains unsolved – he had not passed the landlord or his wife and gone to another part of the public area, he had not gone up the stairs, nor could he have left the building because the doors were still locked. This ghostly visitor did not speak, nor did he give any indication as to who he was. It remains a mystery that may never be solved.

five

The General and the Sister

Officially opened in October 1890 by the Duke of Portland, for many years Mansfield's General Hospital stood at the top of West Hill Drive dispensing care and treatment to the men, women and children of the district.

The King's Mill Hospital and Mansfield's General Hospital shared the treatment of patients – some forms of illnesses and injuries were treated at one hospital while other types were cared for at the other. 'The General', as it was known, is perhaps best remembered not only for its accident and emergency facilities, but also it's care of sick and poorly children, both as outpatients who came for treatment during the daytime and inpatients who were to stay in hospital for a longer period of time.

The derelict Mansfield General Hospital.

The top floor of the General was Robin Hood Ward, the children's ward. The medical staff on the ward were, in some respects, an extended family to those they cared for and were, for a short time, the guardians of those children; a task they took seriously.

Watching over the doctors, nurses and patients of Robin Hood Ward was someone who took their role as guardian more seriously than most. This person was often seen sitting near a doorway just off the ward and although she did not speak to the staff, she faithfully looked after the children, especially at night time. The 'Grey Sister', as she became known, would sit at the side of the door to the sluice room, which in turn was at the side of the door that led onto the ward. It was said that this lady was a former nursing sister who had accidentally administered an overdose of medicine to a child – who subsequently died – and that she was so distraught at her mistake that she took her own life by throwing herself from the sluice room window. Whoever this lady was and whatever the circumstances of her passing, she certainly showed a caring side to her nature, especially if a seriously ill child was on the ward.

At night time two nurses looked after approximately thirty children, but with the quiet of the ward broken only by the sound of the children sleeping, they knew that they had a helping hand close by. If one of the children was in need of attention, the Grey Sister would make herself known by gently tugging at the sleeve of the nurse's uniform. It did not matter whether it was something as simple as the bedding falling from a child or something more serious, the Grey Sister would let them know.

It was on Robin Hood Ward, on the top floor, that the Grey Sister went about her duties.

One particular night, the nurse on duty was making sure that all her patients were settled and that everything was as it should be. As she stood at the end of the row of beds her attention was caught by a movement from the foot of one of the beds. To her surprise she saw the clipboard holding the patients notes rise up and hover in mid-air, as if some invisible doctor or nurse was reading the information. The startled nurse then watched as the same thing happened at the foot of each successive bed.

As helpful and kind as this ghostly spirit was, some of the staff were frightened by her actions and were so disturbed that mediums were called onto the ward to sit with them, while others insisted that a police officer stay with them when they were on night duty. This did not bother our friendly ghost, however, and she was often seen by the mediums and policemen as she sat in her usual place outside the sluice room door. On occasions the door would not stay closed, so in an attempt to rectify the problem new locks were fitted, but all to no avail. The door would unlock itself and gently swing open. On the ward lights would turn on and off by themselves. Not everyone saw the sister as a threat and far from being scared of her, some of the nurses had an affection and trust for her and they realised she was helping out in her own way. Two stories in particular show the caring nature of this earth-bound spirit and how she tried to look after her charges.

One small boy aged about six was admitted to the Robin Hood Ward at the General and, after receiving treatment over a period of time, he was at last discharged. Over the next four or five years he was a frequent visitor to the hospital and was sadly admitted on an all-too-regular basis. Each time he was taken onto the ward he always insisted on being put in the same bed, the one next to the ward entrance door, which in turn was next to the sluice room door. Eventually one of the nurses gently asked the child why he requested the same bed each time, and his reply was quite sincere. He told of how a lady wearing a grey coat brought him sweets, would provide him with drinks, take him to the toilet and, most poignantly, that she was his friend. The nurse understood and he was always allowed to sleep in 'that' bed.

The second tale is a much more remarkable one and was witnessed by more than one person, so its creditability seems to be beyond doubt.

A poorly little girl was admitted onto the ward suffering from an illness that could not be diagnosed, so, to give her more privacy, she was placed in a side ward. At this time parents were unable to stay with their children in hospital because the facilities simply did not exist, and so in the evening the staff took over the role of caring parents as well as those of medical staff. The plight of the little girl so touched the heart of the doctor treating her that each night for the next three months he would sit at the side of her bed reading medical textbooks in an attempt to find the cause of her sickness and thus a cure. The mystery illness gradually took its toll on the girl until, at last, her body could take no more and sadly she died. One of the nurses on duty knew how fond the doctor had become of his patient and, knowing that he was tending to other patients in another part of the hospital, she decided to break the news of the girl's death to him. Managing to locate him and speak to him on the telephone the nurse asked the doctor if he would like to come and say one final goodbye to his young friend, which naturally he did. Arriving on the ward in time to speak to the little girl's parents, the doctor then asked the nurse if the girl's flowers had been attended to. Each hospital has its own ways in dealing with death, especially with that of a child, and the custom at the General was to place a red flower in one hand of the child and a white flower in the other, then to cross the child's arms over their chest and to finally place a red and a white flower in their hair.

No one had as at yet taken on the responsibility of buying any flowers, so, with the screens drawn around the girl's bed, the doctor willingly set off to find this floral tribute to a departed friend.

On his return, the doctor quietly went behind the screen to say his goodbye. However, after quite some time, the nurses on the ward started to wonder why he was taking such a long time to carry out the task; was he finding his mission more difficult than they realised? When he eventually emerged from behind the privacy of the partition he was still carrying the flowers and, when asked why he had been so long, he said that he had been talking with a lady in grey. The flowers did not need to be left with the little girl because someone had already given her some, but who? None of the nurses had left the ward to fetch any and no one had come onto the ward with any flowers, and, more to the point, no one apart from the doctor had gone behind the screen to see the little girl.

Was the Grey Sister the only ghost haunting Mansfield General Hospital?

When it came for the children's ward to be transferred to the King's Mill Hospital, the old Robin Hood Ward at the General became the orthopaedic ward and was renamed the Portland Ward. This new unit was usually empty at night time and staff on the lower floors would hear crying and a plaintiff voice calling out, asking where the children had gone. The calls for the children and the sound of someone walking up and down the corridors went on for years until the General was closed. Sadly, the Grey Sister has not found her way to the King's Mill Hospital to carry on her work, but it is to be hoped that she has at last found some peace.

The Grey Sister was not the only spectral figure to walk the wards and corridors of the General. On Hollins Ward the night staff often saw the ghostly shape of a woman wearing a long grey dress that reminded them of an old-fashioned nurse's uniform. She would walk down the ward quietly and with purpose in her stride before disappearing before their eyes.

The nurses also spoke of how they would be forewarned of the death of a patient. The air would become heavy with the strong smell of pipe tobacco, which would linger for a while before suddenly dispersing as if it had never been there. Shortly afterwards one of the patients would die.

six

Sherwood Forest and the Phantom Couple

herwood Forest is famous throughout the world for Robin Hood, his merry
men and of course Maid Marion, along with a fair smattering of tales about their
adventures with the Sheriff of Nottingham. Running a close second in popularity
comes the Major Oak, the famous tree often associated (perhaps incorrectly) with the
famous outlaw and his followers who, if legend is true, used the forest as their home.
During the early thirteenth century, Sherwood Forest covered about 100,000 acres of
land, which was approximately one fifth of the total size of Nottinghamshire, and this
vast area attracted many of England's monarchs who used it as their private hunting
ground. The harsh punishment imposed for taking anything from the King's forest

MAJOR OAK,   AGE 1,500 YEARS. GIRTH 35 FEET, BASE 64 FEET.

The Major Oak in 1904. (Mansfield Museum)

An early postcard showing the Major Oak. (Mansfield Museum)

without permission meant that in times of want the country-dwelling peasants lived in fear of either starvation or severe retribution if caught stealing or poaching.

For hundreds of years the country folk lived with the dread of being punished not only by the laws of the king but by those of a supernatural being that they believe existed deep within the woodland. Lurking in the forest was the Green Man, a pagan deity who protected the plants and was believed to be a symbol of rebirth. He lurked everywhere and watched everyone. So powerful was the belief in the Green Man that his effigy was placed in churches and can still be seen today with leaves and branches surrounding his head and face like an all-enveloping shroud.

For many years parts of Sherwood Forest were avoided both day and night because it was supposed that an invisible being lay in wait there, giving those that passed the sensation they were being strangled, while others have seen strange figures in the trees. For the sceptic, all of these sightings can be explained as encounters with wild creatures or wild imaginations, but for one Forest Ranger his experience was all too real.

In the late 1980s the Ranger was in a remote part of Sherwood Forest going about his everyday duties well away from the hustle and bustle of the Major Oak and the visitor centre near Edwinstowe. Taking a few moments to look around and listen to the birds, he saw in front of him some yards away a man and woman who he described as a loving couple. The man wore an old-style hat and long coat, while the woman's most striking feature was her hairstyle, which was reminiscent of the 1940s; in fact both the man and woman looked as if they had stepped out of a history book whose

The Green Man of Sherwood Forest.

pages had been turned to that decade. For a second the Ranger's attention was drawn to the sound of a bird at his side, yet when he looked back the couple had vanished. For a while the Ranger thought nothing of the incident, until he realised the couple were walking in an area where no footpath existed and the vegetation was too dense to be able to walk, as the couple had been.

Sherwood Forest, where a ghostly couple have been seen.

The incident passed into obscurity until two or three years later, when it was brought sharply back into focus with another sighting. Deep fissures had opened up in the forest caused by natural geological activity, and workmen set about digging down to the bedrock to make repairs. In an area near to where the visitor centre was later built, one contractor was steadily working away late one night in an attempt to get the work completed as speedily as possible. At about midnight the contractor, who was busy in his digger, watched in disbelief as a man and woman walked right through the area in which he was working without taking any notice of him. His description of the couple exactly matched the one given by the Ranger earlier. The shaken workman returned to work the next morning vowing never to return there again on his own.

This new sighting reminded the Ranger of his encounter with the couple and aroused his curiosity. He remembered that during the Second World War the army had used Sherwood Forest as one huge army camp, with buildings and ammunition dumps littering the woods, and many paths made as the army personnel went from one part of the forest to another. Armed with this knowledge the Ranger went back to the area of the original sighting and there he found a footpath – heavily overgrown with vegetation and with trees growing where the path had once been. It had been unusable as a pathway for many years, yet this is where he had seen the couple. Were they lovers from the war years taking a stroll down memory lane? Who knows?

seven

The Restless Spirits of Annesley Hall

When Lord Byron left the shores of his homeland in 1816 and headed onto the continent, he left behind many memories of a life that had been at times turbulent and at others touched with tenderness. During his young and formative years Byron had grown close to Mary Chaworth, whose family owned Annesley Hall, but alas this love affair seemed doomed to failure. Both families had for a long time borne each other a degree of malice that seemed to stem from a tragic and needless event that happened some years before.

Byron's predecessor, the 5th Baron, had gained the epithet of 'The Wicked Lord' or 'Devil Baron' because of his eccentric, and at times violent and largely unsavoury character; there was even talk of insanity. It was one particular incident that led to the death of one of the story's protagonists.

In a poorly lit room at the Star and Garter Tavern in London, William Byron and William Chaworth entered into a heated discussion over the best way to hang game such as pheasants and other creatures. Such was the disagreement that Byron challenged Chaworth to a duel over the matter and with swords drawn the two began fighting for their lives with the 'Wicked Lord' being hailed as the victor when he ran Chaworth through the abdomen. As Chaworth lay on the floor dying, he is said to have complained that the poor light in the room was the true reason for him losing the fight. Byron was arrested and charged with murder, but to the horror of the dead man's family he was found guilty of the lesser crime of manslaughter, whereupon he was duly fined and set free. To make matters worse, Byron had the murder weapon mounted on a wall inside Newstead Abbey itself. It is also said that on another occasion the 'Wicked Lord' got into an argument with his coachman, whereupon Bryon promptly shot the man, put his body in the coach and drove the carriage himself. With all this history, the omens did not fare well for the young Mary Chaworth and the poet, and when the young Byron visited Annesley Hall one day he was devastated when he overheard Mary telling a relative that she would not consider the prospect of marrying him (others say it was Mary's family who blocked any form of union). The heartbroken Byron left to pursue his own life while Mary eventually married John Musters in a marriage that was less than happy.

December 1831 was a momentous month for Mary as her youngest son, Charles, set sail on HMS *Beagle* on a voyage of discovery that would change the world, and would lead one of those on board, Charles Darwin, to question how life on Earth

The haunted Annesley Hall gatehouse.

began and would eventually lead to his revolutionary theory on evolution. It was also a voyage that would see mother and son parted forever as tragic events on both sides of the world would dramatically show. This twelve-year-old boy was liked by the whole crew and was very quickly taken to their hearts as the ship got into its daily routine. By May 1832, HMS *Beagle* had reached Bahia in South America and a landing party, including young Charles, was sent ashore. Within days of their return it was obvious that some of the men were seriously ill, Charles being one of those struck down, and it was decided that a change of air would speed their recovery. The *Beagle* put to sea, but alas, two of the landing party died, among them young Charles Musters. Such was the sadness over the death of Charles that Captain Fitzroy, captain of the *Beagle*, and Charles Darwin both wrote of their distress over the boy's death, a particularly sad event since only three days before his own passing Charles had been informed of his mother's death. Mary had died back in England of rheumatic fever, while her son had succumbed to malaria in South America.

Many believe that Mary and her former suitor, Lord Byron, haunt Annesley Hall and that she can be seen walking in and around her old bedroom as well as walking through walls on the ground floor. Charles is also thought to be there with his mother, yet he is less content as stones and other objects are thrown at people nearby. The 'Wicked Lord' Byron's spirit is thought to haunt the cellars.

Many people have described seeing the figure of a hooded monk dressed in a dense black garb in the churchyard of the long since abandoned and ruined church that lies close to the Hall, while others have reported seeing this same figure crossing the road outside. On more than one occasion motorists have been horrified to see this frightening figure step out in front of their vehicle, before vanishing at the point of impact. One night a lady driver witnessed the car in front of her pass right through a shadowy figure, a shape she described as being like a swirling dress that floated in the air. The sight so frightened her that she drove home at high speed without stopping for the traffic lights, which were on red, to change. Is it really the ghost of a monk they see, or is it some other lost soul? There has never been a monastery at Annesley, but Newstead Abbey is just a short distance away and perhaps the monk is making his way there. Or perhaps he is heading for Felley Priory, which is only about two miles away.

The church next to Annesley Hall, where a spectral monk was seen.

The church next to Annesley Hall.

The ruined Annesley Hall gatehouse.

The ruined Victorian wing.

Felley Priory was founded in 1156 by Ralph Britto, Lord of Annesley, for Augustinians Canons, otherwise known as Black Canons. Perhaps the monk is making his way back home after visiting his Lord and patron.

The shape of a young woman also makes herself known in a number of locations – but is it the same woman in each place? One young lady is seen sitting at the side of a nearby well and has even been seen to rise from inside the well itself. Is she the poor soul that was found dead inside this well many years ago and, if so, how did she die? Did she take her own life or was it taken from her? If her death was suicide then it was not the only one at the Hall, for a young serving girl hanged herself inside the building after suffering at the hands of a man. Visitors have often seen the face of a young woman looking out of the windows, perhaps watching to see if her abuser is returning.

There is also the sad tale of the discovery of the bodies of a mother and baby found buried under the stairs while repair work was taking place at the Hall. Someone had buried them in a secretive way – was it their killer or someone with a secret to hide? Perhaps the woman is the ghost that walks the rooms?

Many ghosts and spirits reside at Annesley Hall, which is why it is renowned as one of the most haunted locations in the country.

eight

The Old Forest Glade School

L ike many old buildings that had outlived their original purpose, the Old Forest Glade school on Mansfield Road in Sutton-in-Ashfield gained a new lease of life when it was converted for use by businesses. Never again would schoolchildren run around in the playground as they took their break from schoolwork, from now on it would be the sound of machinery that would fill the air, bringing with it the air of prosperity. For Lilian Wishaw, the proprietor of a local hosiery firm, the chance to move into the premises, which were centrally located and close to all major transport routes, was an opportunity too good to miss. In early 1985, Mrs Wishaw moved her business into the part of the old school that had at one time been a large storage area, the caretaker's office and the school toilets. Its use and layout had now been changed to accommodate a centrally placed main work area, to the right of which was a packing area, the rest room and, finally, on the extreme right, the staff toilets. To the left of the work area was the factory shop and reception, the main office and, beyond this, a storage area. For security reasons, each of the rooms had lockable doors that were fitted with deadbolts to ensure maximum protection when the factory was closed. The design of the building worked well and with new electrics throughout, there was no reason why work could not start on the manufacture of new garments. Soon the factory was up and running, with production running smoothly and orders being fulfilled.

Occasionally there was the odd minor hiccup, but this was put down to the sort of teething trouble that all new machinery seems to get every now and then. However, odd things began to happen that could not be explained. The first incident of any significance occurred in the main machine room, when one of the electrical cables that powered the lights exploded like a firework. There was no advance warning of this potential catastrophe and when the manager, Philip Sanders, who had witnessed the whole incident, called in professional electricians to repair the damage, he was surprised to hear there was no underlying problem. Over the next few months the cables continued to explode and each time they were repaired the electricians could find to reason why it had happened.

As the weeks and months passed, more strange things occurred, each one causing increasing bewilderment to those who witnessed them or had to put right any damage. Machinery would break down with a whole variety of faults, such as drive shafts snapping or gears breaking, and the engineers who repaired the faults, just like the electricians, could offer no rational reason for what had happened, particularly as some of the machines were new and all of them were maintained to a high standard. Garment patterns would disappear from their storage place and reappear later on; production line tickets would also disappear and reappear some time later. Files and documents would go missing from the main office, sometimes one sheet from a file and sometimes the whole file would go, only to be returned to their rightful place days later. Was it possible that a member of staff was tampering with all the paperwork and documents, or was it just a case of inefficiency? It was certainly something that had to be considered, but the lady running the office had come with impeccable references and her work was of a high standard. In an attempt to alleviate any potential problems, the staff were retrained in procedures and monitoring took place, but still papers disappeared and records went missing.

Members of staff started to feel that they were being watched, or that someone was standing near them when nobody else was around, and occasionally they complained that they felt as though they were not alone when they were in the toilet block. In the packing room and in parts of the main machine room the temperature would drop so much that the heating had to be put on – even during the summer months.

Despite all these strange happenings in the factory, productivity was high with large orders to fulfil and the morale of the workers buoyant. The unusual events were not worrying the staff too much, especially with such a 'hands-on' approach by the owner

The old Forest Glade School, where strange and unexplained events took place in the buildings behind.

and manager, yet even this type of approach by Mrs Wishaw and Mr Sanders could not fail to stop some from wondering about the fault with the telephone.

To make sure no important telephone calls were missed, a telephone extension bell had been fitted inside the machine room to alert the management of any calls. Imagine everyone's surprise when, on occasions, the extension bell started to ring continuously. If the telephone was answered when the bell rang non-stop, no one would be on the line at the other end, and, in one instance, when the bell was ringing, Mr Sanders unplugged the telephone and carried it into the work area, only to find the bell still ringing, which should have been impossible, because the single line switchboard powered the bell through the telephone. The telephone engineers were called to check out the circuits and, just as the electricians and machine mechanics had said before, nothing wrong could be found.

A lot of mysterious events also took place while the factory was closed for the night, when the building was locked and secure and everyone was at home. In the mornings many machines would have been re-threaded with yarn in a completely ad-hoc manner, as if someone had been playing a practical joke. One morning, when the factory was opened up, an unbelievable sight met the eyes of the owner and manager, thousands and thousands of metres of new yarns were wound round and round the machinery and all the way up to the rafters and its supports, with more of the yarns spread around on the floor. The cones from which the yarn had been unwound lay scattered around the floor and the whole mess provided an impenetrable tangle that looked like a gigantic spider's web. The police were called in case it had been a break-in, however investigations proved that this was not the case, no locks had been forced, no padlocks had been damaged and all internal bolts were still in place and secure. Mice and rats were also discounted simply because a factory of this nature had to be very careful about rodents damaging their stock. As far as the police were concerned it was a complete mystery.

It was common practice for hosiery factories to have a full shut down at lunchtime on Fridays so that work could start afresh on Monday. Machines were to be checked and the complete area fully cleaned; when this was finished a visual check from the management to make sure everything was alright would signify the end of work. On one particular weekend it was necessary to make some deliveries to a number of important clients, so Mrs Wishaw and Mr Sanders thought it best to split the deliveries over the Saturday and Sunday. Saturday's deliveries to Yorkshire went well and, with the prospect of a long trip to Essex on the Sunday, they decided to make an early start. Arriving at the factory early on the Sunday morning they were met by the sight of the external door swinging open. Fearing a break-in, they carefully approached the factory, wondering if the intruders were still on site. Relieved to find that they were alone, they called the police. Yet they found that there had been no break-in, there could not have been, because the open door had been secured by large bolts from the *inside* and all the internal doors within the factory still had the bolts and deadlocks on and the main entrance door was still locked. The machine room was once again a scene of total disruption, with yet another enormous spider's web of yarns covering the whole room.

With the police investigation hitting a brick wall, Mrs Wishaw was pleased to receive a visit on the following Monday from an old school friend of hers who had joined the police force and was now in the CID. He advised her to call in a medium to see if they could help her out as he felt it was not an earthly presence causing the problem. At about 2 p.m. that afternoon, Mrs Wishaw was helping one of the ladies sort out a problem on her machine when the woman let out a scream, there was a gust of air as if the wind was blowing, and then Mrs Wishaw saw what appeared to be a young girl of about seven years of age wearing a duffel coat and black wellingtons run past them towards the toilet area.

Mr Sanders also saw the little girl in the factory. He had decided to sweep the floor of the toilet block and was just completing his task when he became aware that someone was coming towards him from the machine room. His own words best describe what happened next:

… as I looked up I saw the figure of a young girl, probably aged about ten years. Her appearance was more opaque than transparent and she was wearing a green school blazer with badge or emblem I could not describe, with a white shirt and a tie that appeared to be dark blue with lighter blue stripes diagonally across the tie with a dark grey pleated skirt, white knee-length socks showing above dark grey Wellington boots. Her hair appeared brown and shoulder length with slight waves to the sides. She was skipping forward but throwing her legs side to side as she skipped forward; she was giggling and laughing in a happy manner. She skipped and laughed her way toward me and I stood frozen to the spot seemingly unable to move, there was no fear, in fact it was a strange feeling, one of being numb. She approached me and then to my surprise passed straight through my body, turning into the middle of the three toilets, as she did her laughter was so full of joy, so full of fun, like a child enjoying playing a practical joke. She continued into the toilet and passed right through the back wall of the toilet, which led directly to the outside of the building into the church grounds next door to our building, at which point her laughter was even more happy and more playful like that of a very happy child, after a few seconds the situation was quickly normal again. My reaction was witnessed and although I never saw or heard her again, I can today visualise the event as clear as the day it happened …

These last incidents convinced Mrs Wishaw to contact a medium friend of hers to help her out and try to get to the bottom of things once and for all. The medium arrived, prepared to move the mischievous child on, but as she started her work the child started to fight back and more than one person heard a child's voice saying, 'I don't want to go'. In the end the medium was satisfied that the child was gone and indeed the number of strange happenings dropped dramatically, but the identity of the child was a puzzle that Mrs Wishaw wanted to solve. Managing to trace a former headmistress of the school, she was able to discover that a child of a similar age to the one that had been seen had drowned in a swimming pool. The headmistress refused to give any more details. For over two years the child had played tricks on the workforce until at last she was gone, but one question remained – who was she?

nine

King's Mill Hospital and 'Hank the Yank'

The mainstay for hospital treatment for Mansfield, Ashfield and the surrounding district is King's Mill Hospital, a huge complex of treatment rooms and wards that can deal with a vast range of ailments ranging from the smallest of problems right up to major operations and long-term illnesses. For generations this site has dispensed care and understanding to those that pass through its doors, and yet its beginnings were, by comparison, far more humble.

Britain had virtually stood alone against Nazi Germany until America joined the conflict, after it was attacked by Japan at Pearl Harbour in December 1941. With war raging around the world, America sent thousands of its soldiers and airmen to Britain, and with them came the need for a system of support that could cope with this sudden influx. Even before the United States entered into the conflict, the British government had realised the need for a large increase in medical facilities and in August 1940

An aerial view of King's Mill Hospital in 1956.

Nottinghamshire County Council met with the Ministry of Health regarding plans to build Sutton Emergency Hospital. The farmland known as Grange Farm smallholdings, which was owned by the council, was deemed suitable and permission was granted for building work to begin. The Ministry of Works for the Emergency Medical Services had taken steps to plan the new hospital and its construction took place from 1941-2 on the site of the long-established farm. It was believed that Mansfield and Ashfield were among the safer places in war-torn England and the chances of enemy action were minimal, allowing for a more peaceful environment for the patients to recuperate. The new Sutton Emergency Hospital was to be the first US Army hospital built in England during the Second World War. Construction was still in progress when the first US personnel arrived in June 1942.

With its frontage looking towards King's Mill reservoir, the main central corridor of the new hospital traced its way backwards up the gentle slope of the hill behind, with the wards leading off to the side, much like a herringbone. Many years later a bronze plaque would be placed in the main entrance foyer, proudly proclaiming that it had been the '30th General Hospital of the University of California'. Not only was the new hospital intended to treat sick and wounded US servicemen, it was also to be used to treat allied personnel and enemy prisoners of war. Next to the hospital was a prisoner of war camp used to house Italian prisoners, for whom the war had ended. Any prisoners that received treatment at the hospital were immediately sent to the camp once they were thought to be fit enough.

In 1942 an aircraft landed in a nearby field (this later became the home of Sutton Harrier Athletic Club) and the officer inside made his way to the hospital, where he visited the sick. The surprise visitor was Clarke Gable, the Hollywood film star who was in England to make a motion picture, and his morale-boosting visits were thought essential in helping the recovery of the wounded.

Many sick and injured service personnel were looked after by the military doctors and nurses over the next three years; some of the wounded were horribly disfigured and mutilated but the medical staff carried on, diligently working to ease their suffering. With the preparations for D-Day well advanced, the 30th General Hospital left in May 1944 to ready themselves for the invasion of France, where they would set up field hospitals. It was left to the new occupants, the 184th General Hospital, to fill the void and carry on as before. After the D-Day landings, the hospital was full to bursting point with around 1,000 injured military personnel filling every available space, while staff at the hospital carried on under extreme pressure to tend to their needs.

As the war drew to a close in 1945, it became clear that the US forces would have no more need for the Sutton Emergency Hospital and so, shortly after VE-Day, they departed, leaving the buildings intact.

For two years the site remained empty until, in 1947, the Home Office took over the site from the Ministry of Health and it became the 'No. 3 Police Training Centre'. The first people to see inside the old hospital were surprised to find that the American's had left behind a lot of equipment and personal effects. The stripped, metal-framed beds were still there, so were many inventories and records, as well as personal letters, boots and other items. It was as if the previous occupants had left in a hurry. The new training centre's time at the old hospital was to be short-lived and by January 1951 they had moved out, leaving the way clear for a new hospital to be opened for the people in the area. It was when the National Health Service took over the site from the Home Office that the name King's Mill was adopted, a title by which it would be forever known.

The official opening of the new hospital came in September of the same year, when just one part of the complex (to begin with just three wards) was put into use. The rest of the site would take a lot of expensive and extensive repairs to make it usable once again, a time-consuming and lengthy process. Slowly but surely the size and scope of the facilities that were made available grew as each part of the old complex was brought back up to standard. As the patients began to use the ever-increasing range of services, the staff settled in to a tried and tested routine, however something was not quite right, something was beginning to disturb the workforce.

Ward 13 was situated on the left of the main corridor, just above another ward that was to become known as Nightingale Ward, and it was here that strange and unexplained events took place. In the linen room the smell of cigar smoke would fill the air and a strange, cold presence would overcome anyone in there. Some felt a hand on their shoulder, sensed they were not alone, and the door handle would rattle on its own. Over the coming years a ghostly shape was seen floating along the main corridor between Ward 13 and the operating theatre. Tradition has it that this solitary phantom is that of an American serviceman who died shortly after an operation, and that he is wandering the corridor searching for his amputated limb. Others say that the serviceman walks the corridor because his body had been left behind in the mortuary when the US forces moved out.

The story of 'Hank the Yank', as the ghost became known, gained some credence in 1967 when one of the local women – who had become a GI bride – paid a return visit to the town following the death of her mother. While sitting in a Mansfield Woodhouse pub, she got talking to a young nurse who worked at King's Mill Hospital. The conversation soon turned to the odd events that took place around Ward 13, and, with her curiosity roused, the visitor asked the nurse if she could see this 'haunted' ward. Duly obliging, the nurse took the visitor to see the place where it all happened, telling her that she and her colleagues were so wary of 'Hank' that they would not walk there alone. She then pointed to a toilet doorway that had been boarded up, claiming that this was the place that 'Hank' had actually died after taking his own life because of his injuries.

'Hank', it appears, was not the only ghost or apparition at the hospital, in one area known as the Clinical Illustrations Department, items would find their way onto the centre of the floor when the staff were away on photo shoots, even though the door was securely locked. When the room was empty, unusual noises could be heard emanating from inside, while occasionally the sound of footsteps going into the room were heard when in fact no one could be seen.

On the children's ward a nurse on night duty heard a young boy crying. As she made her way over to him, the crying stopped. Asking if she could help him, the boy replied that there was no need because the other nurse had sorted things out. The nurse was puzzled because she was the only one on duty.

The main corridor of King's Mill Hospital, where 'Hank' has been seen.

In other parts of the hospital members of staff heard their names called out when they were alone, bin lids would be lifted up and down by invisible hands, doors that were propped open would have the wedges knocked out and then shut by themselves, and disembodied legs were seen walking past doors.

The former Duke Elder and Bert Ashworth Wards also had their fair share of extraordinary occurrences. Doors were heard to open and close even when no windows were open to allow a draught. At other times staff heard the sound of footsteps coming from the end of the ward when nobody was there, and the sound could not have come from the corridor outside because the doors were firmly closed. As elsewhere in the hospital, the smell of tobacco sometimes rent the air, while at other times anyone nearby would feel a firm tap on the shoulder, only to discover that there was no one nearby.

Nor did the main corridor escape the attention of one ghost, who gave the impression of being in a hurry. Fast-moving footsteps were heard rushing up the corridor behind one male member of staff: when he turned to see who it was he was taken aback to see that he was alone. However, with the sound of the footsteps growing louder and faster, he automatically stepped to one side to allow the unseen spectre pass, which, to his surprise, continued past him and, more remarkably, caused a rush of air that he could feel. Maybe 'Hank' was not alone in his wanderings of this long, narrow corridor.

One of the wards of the old military hospital.

The 'H' block of King's Mill Hospital.

It could be argued that a wartime hospital is more than likely to have a number of lost souls wandering through the labyrinth of old corridors and wards because of the injuries suffered by servicemen and the torment they endured before they finally slipped away. Equally it could be said that the doctors and nurses who tended to them have stayed to continue their work, but this does not explain one strange incident that took place some years ago.

Set some distance away from the old hospital were some structures know as the 'H' block, simply because that is the shape in which they were constructed. Sometime during the late 1990s or early 2000s, Eve Booker was working inside one of these buildings when something attracted her attention. Looking up, she saw to her surprise a figure walking past the doorway, something that should not have been possible because the external door was closed and access could only be made by using a keypad.

Her colleague later went to the nearby tea bar, only to see what was thought to be the same character walking down the corridor. This unearthly man was described as wearing old style fatigue clothing and boots that were unlaced, however the lower part of his boots were not visible, almost as if they had been cut off. It was pointed out that the floor level had been raised slightly since the time of the old military hospital and that the man in fatigues was walking on the old floor. The same serviceman was also seen walking through a bricked-up doorway as he made his way to some unknown destination.

Now that the last vestiges of the 30th General Hospital of the University of California have all but gone, it is to be hoped that those long gone men and women who drifted through its passages and wards can at last depart in peace.

ten

Lord Byron and the Black Friar

Newstead Abbey has a tumultuous past that would appear to be the work of a fiction writer at his most outrageous. With stories of royal patronage, religious persecution, eccentric owners, scandal and ghosts that walk the corridors of the house, it seems that this place has it all.

The abbey dates back many centuries to about the year 1170, when Henry II decided to set up a priory in the heart of Sherwood Forest, not far from the Abbeys of Welbeck and Rufford. His main reason for doing so was most probably as a way of placating the religious orders and populace after the disastrous episode over the murder of the Archbishop of Canterbury, Thomas Becket. Whether Henry actually wanted Becket killed or whether it was the words of a drunken man that uttered that fateful phrase, 'Will no one rid me of this turbulent priest?' will never be known, but, regardless, Henry had to make amends very quickly or risk losing his throne.

With the abbey founded as an Augustinian priory, the religious men inside its walls set about their duties finding favour from many wealthy and powerful men over

A 1905 view of Newstead Abbey.

the centuries. King John confirmed their lands and even made them larger, while other benefactors added to their wealth and influence, a process that would carry on for many years. By the time of Henry VIII, Newstead, like the majority of religious houses, had the sort of wealth that made them the envy of many a noble family and it was this wealth that was to be their ultimate downfall. Henry VIII had become increasingly alienated from the Pope and the Catholic faith until he finally proclaimed himself the head of the Church in England and made the split from Rome. This gave the king the opportunity to close and plunder all the religious houses in the country and in 1539 Newstead Abbey succumbed to the inevitable. The following year the church and priory were given by the king to Sir John Byron of Colwick, Lieutenant of Sherwood Forest. This, it seems, is when the Goblin Friar started to make his terrifying appearances.

As the Dissolution of the Monasteries took place throughout the land, legend has it that as the Abbot of Newstead was forcibly taken from his cell and evicted from the building he placed a curse on anyone would should live in his former home. He even cursed the building itself, and the well from which the water was drawn was not spared either. The Goblin Friar, also known as the Black Friar, was said to appear to the head of the Byron family as a portent of doom and during the years of the Byron ownership he certainly made his presence known.

Perhaps the most famous victim of the Black Friar was Lord George Gordon Byron, the famous poet, who saw this fearsome spectre on more than one occasion. In one particular instance Byron was asleep in his bedchamber when he was woken from his slumber by the sensation of someone, or something, climbing onto the bed. As he opened his eyes he saw in front of him a large black shape, completely featureless except for two glowing red eyes. The apparition then rolled off the bed and onto the floor before vanishing.

Probably the most prophetic visitation of the Black Friar to Byron was a short time before his marriage to Anne Millbanke, when the portent of doom made his appearance once again. The prophecy became real when the marriage failed miserably after about fifteen months amid allegations of cruel and indecent behaviour. Byron left the country never to return.

For all the ill-fortune the Black Monk brought to the Bryon family, it would seem that he did have a softer side for those in distress or need, and, as one incident showed, his help proved invaluable. One day in the 1930s, a woman from the village of Newstead was close to giving birth and her husband telephoned the doctor, fearing that time was getting short. The doctor travelled as fast as he could but was unable to find his way to the house until at last he saw what appeared to be a man in a monks garb standing by the waterfall in the grounds of the abbey. When the doctor stopped to ask the way, the figure simply lifted an arm and pointed in the direction the doctor should take. Fortunately for both the woman and her husband, the doctor arrived just in time to help with the birth. Asking the man for directions had been a stroke of luck, not least because there had been no monks living in the area for centuries.

In 1818 Thomas Wildman bought the abbey from Lord Byron and began restoring the house. As the Wildmans turned the abbey into their home, Sophie Hyatt, a lady described as being both deaf and dumb, moved into Weir Mill farmhouse in the grounds. Poor Sophie was shy and retiring; she avoided meeting others and carried a slate with her at all times so that she could communicate with those she chose to meet. An avid fan of the Lord Byron, she soon gained the name of the 'White Lady' as she always wore pale or light-coloured clothing.

With insufficient funds to look after herself, Sophie relied heavily on a relative to support her, but tragedy struck when the relative died. In an attempt to gain an income from another relative, she decided to head to London to seek help. Leaving a note for the Wildmans, she set off to catch the London coach from Nottingham. Sophie did not realise just how fond of her the Wildmans were and when they read the note they immediately sent a rider to catch her up and to ask her to return. It was their intention to provide Sophie with suitable accommodation for the rest of her life.

Sadly the rider reached Nottingham too late: as Sophie crossed the road in the Market Square she was hit by a horse and cart and died. The driver of the cart had shouted a warning but poor deaf Sophie was unable to hear anything and she stepped into the path of the horse.

It is said that she still walks the paths at Newstead – visitors to the abbey have reported a white misty shape while others have seen Sophie's ghost passing through the walls of some of the rooms.

Sophie Hyatt is not the only spirit seen in the grounds, for a large dog has been seen wandering about. Is this the ghost of Boatswain, Lord Byron's faithful dog? Byron was so taken by Boatswain he asked that when he died he be buried with his favourite dog, which he had already buried in the grounds of the abbey with a magnificent monument put up in commemoration. The poet's wishes were never fulfilled, so could Boatswain and Sophie Hyatt both be searching for Lord Byron, a man they both loved in their own particular way?

Should you visit Newstead Abbey keep an eye out for Sophie and Boatswain, but do not try to approach the dog for he will simply disappear in front of your eyes, and beware the black Rooks for these, it is claimed, are the souls of the Black Monks who have been reborn as birds and have returned to keep an eye on the abbey and its inhabitants.

eleven

The Old Chapel

Every day hundreds of pedestrians and drivers travel along Shirebrook's Main Street, busily going about their everyday lives as they visit any one of the shops and businesses that line both sides of the road or make their way to another part of the town. However, do any of those travellers appreciate the little gem that stands just a few yards back from the main road? Over the centuries Shirebrook has grown from a tiny little hamlet to a much larger conurbation that at one time relied heavily on the coal mining industry for its prosperity, while now its attention has turned elsewhere. A quick glance at any old map shows just how much the place has changed – Sanderson's 1835 map 'Twenty Miles round Mansfield' shows just a few scattered houses along the main road. Take a closer look at the map, however, and you will see a drawing of a building inside a tiny square with the simple inscription 'chapel' beside it. This ancient building is believed to have dated back to the fourteenth century, or earlier, and had been in use for many years until it fell into disrepair during the seventeenth century. After extensive renovations a century later, it once again fell into decline and was finally demolished. A larger church was built to replace it, and in September 1843 Holy Trinity Church was consecrated.

For some of the locals the new church was of little use to them simply because they did not follow the faith that was preached there, so a new place of worship had to be planned. In 1847 James Needham, his wife Elizabeth and a number of other worshipers from the local area took possession of a piece of land at the side of the new church and built their own Methodist Chapel, which was destined to be a place of learning for children as well as a place of worship.

For years the chapel was a place where the faithful could meet and take comfort, but alas, its days as a place of worship drew to a close and after a number of changes it eventually became the local library. Finally, when even that use was outlived, it was converted into a private dwelling. With the conversion completed, the house became home to a successive number of families until, in May 2000, Dean Griffiths took possession and moved in. At first all seemed well, with only a small problem with the heating appearing to mar what was an ideal home. Cold spots would appear in the rooms, especially the bedroom, even when the radiators were turned on high, yet when the heating engineer inspected the system he could find no fault whatsoever. Ornaments then started to move along the shelves and cabinets on which they were standing, all by themselves. Coffee cups were found on the mantelpiece and on the kitchen table – a particularly sore point with Dean as he insists on using coasters to protect the furniture.

Dean was starting to wonder why these odd things were happening when one of the most bizarre events so far took place. Deciding to enjoy some wine, he carefully put an almost full glass down while he went to another room. When he returned the glass had disappeared, and a thorough search of the room failed to find it. To this day neither the glass nor the wine has been found. This finally convinced Dean that he had a ghost in the house and although he was not disturbed by its presence, he thought it better not to tell anyone in case they thought him mad.

A lot of people have a secret place in their house where they keep money safe for a rainy day and Dean also followed that trend, making sure that just enough was safely hidden away to deal with any problems that might crop up. One particular day he realised he would need some money in a hurry, but when he checked his hiding place the money was gone. Obviously he had not used the money himself, so, fearing a robbery, he called the police. After examining the scene the police called in the scenes of crime officers, who fingerprinted the area including the money container, but the only fingerprints they found were that of Dean and so they drew a blank, after all there was no sign of a forced entry. Puzzled and somewhat irritated by this, Dean thought it best to carry on as normal and once again the hiding place was put to use until, six months later, the money vanished yet again. As before there was no evidence of a break-in and no one else knew of the hiding place. As with the missing wine glass, the money was never found and from then on the secret hiding place has not been used and no money is kept in the house.

Shirebrook chapel undergoing repair and conversion into a house. (Dean Griffiths)

The old chapel today.

While he was out one evening, Dean met a previous owner of the house who looked at him knowingly and asked about the ghost at the top of the stairs, he also told the surprised home owner that his dog would not go up the stairs either.

Confirmation of the ghostly visitor came when a guest to the house entered the living room and said someone was at the top of the stairs outside the bathroom. Whatever doubts he had harboured, this was proof to Dean that there was indeed a ghost in the house and that it was not his imagination.

Just after midnight one night he and his friend were in the kitchen enjoying a late meal when the keys in the back door started to move. As the pair watched, the keys moved more and more vigorously, jumping in an up and down motion in the lock. After about twenty seconds the keys gently returned to their normal position.

After a rather eventful period, Dean decided it was time to act and, sitting down on the sofa in the living room, he told his ghost in no uncertain terms that if it did not settle down he would 'have them got rid of'. The occasional unusual thing still takes place but on nothing like the scale of before, so it looks like his spiritual companion has taken heed. No deaths have ever occurred in this old building so it would appear that a former member of the chapel congregation is still looking after the old place; a comforting thought.

twelve

The Ghosts of Bolsover Castle

High on a rocky outcrop overlooking the Vale of Scarsdale stands Bolsover Castle, the seventeenth-century 'pleasure palace' built by the Cavendish family as a monument to wealth, power and the pursuit of entertainment. The present castle, begun in 1612 by Charles Cavendish, the youngest son of the famous Bess of Hardwick, lies on the same site as an ancient medieval castle that had been on that site since at least 1173 and was the scene of a brutal battle in 1215 between the supporters of King John and those of the Barons. By the time Charles Cavendish took possession of Bolsover, the old castle must have been in a poor state of repair for within a short time he had employed Robert Smythson, the finest architect of his time, to design a new edifice that would give the air of a gentleman's house while still managing to retain the look of a traditional castle, yet making use of all the innovative and modern ideas of the day.

Bolsover Castle.

The Little Castle at Bolsover, 1906.

Smythson was at the forefront of his profession and had a great reputation; many of his buildings being designed for the wealthiest of families. Among his works were Wollaton Hall at Nottingham and Hardwick Hall, just a few miles from Bolsover, built for Charles Cavendish's irrepressible mother, Bess. It took only five weeks to demolish the old castle and to begin work on building this new aristocratic reflection of affluence. When work got under way on the new castle Cavendish was approaching his sixtieth birthday, and his desire was to build a place of relaxation and leisure away from the hustle and bustle of the main family home at Welbeck Abbey.

Sadly, in 1617, before the 'Little Castle' was completed, Charles Cavendish died, never seeing his project come to fruition, and everything passed on to his eldest son, William.

William Cavendish was in his mid-twenties and, rather than continue to build the new castle as a residence suitable for retirement, he changed its use to a 'pleasure palace', a place to entertain and enjoy life to the full. In later years he was to become one of Europe's leading swordsmen and horsemen; his skill with the sword making him a man to be feared if brought to anger, while his reputation as a horseman kept him in high regard throughout the land.

When Civil War ravaged the land in the 1640s, Cavendish became commander in chief of all the king's armies north of the Trent and with it came great prestige and responsibility, so much so that after the battle of Marston Moor was lost, he felt duty bound to go into exile. During his self-imposed banishment on the continent, he was able to write a book on horsemanship that brought him even more respect amongst his peers and this remarkable piece of writing is still in print today. Throughout his time away from his beloved homeland, he continued to pursue the pleasures of life by throwing lavish entertainments for the rich and powerful and buying a string of fine horses to indulge himself in his passion for riding, while all this time writing plays and poetry. Among his many acquaintances was the future Charles II, who William Cavendish had been governor to before the war had started.

For sixteen long years his exile continued until finally, in 1660, England rejected Parliamentarian rule and King Charles II was invited to return to the country of his birth and take up his role of monarch. In the wake of his return, the vast number of nobles that had sought refuge abroad also returned, including William Cavendish, Marquis of Newcastle. While away from England, Cavendish had married his second wife, Margaret Lucas, and together they hoped to rebuild not only their lives but also their fortune, which had been lost many years before during the Civil War. For Cavendish himself there were many reasons to return and to restore his previous way of life: not only would he finally be able to make his way home and take up the training of his beloved horses in his own riding school, there was also the prospect of returning to the days of sumptuous entertainment in familiar surroundings.

On 30 July 1634, William Cavendish put on such a spellbinding entertainment at Bolsover Castle it was believed at the time it would never be surpassed. He had invited King Charles I and Queen Henrietta Maria to stay at Welbeck Abbey and, while there, preparations were made to hold a masque at Bolsover in honour the King and Queen. The aristocratic nobility and families of the gentry of Nottinghamshire and Derbyshire were invited to attend, special lace and linen was made to adorn the royal tables, the kitchens worked overtime cooking over 6,500 birds, sturgeon was imported and Ben Jonson, the foremost playwright of his day, was asked to write the masque that was to be performed. To top off this wondrous spectacle two children dressed as cherubs and wearing wings made from silver were lowered from an artificial cloud, carrying food on silver platters for the royal couple.

This was the type of leisure pursuit that William Cavendish lived for; he believed that life was meant to be enjoyed and that the finer things of life should be his.

As you walk up the entrance steps and enter the Little Castle you pass through the servants dining quarters and into a small passageway where, to your left, is a room which is decorated in black and gold around its ornate wooden panelling. There have been many reports of men being kicked in this room by an unseen foot and there have been sightings of a ghostly figure standing next to the fireplace. On one occasion a group of photographic students set up their equipment to take a shot of the fireplace, there was a flash from their camera, a second after-flash and, as the second flash died away, the figure of a man appeared in front of them. The students and lecturer left the room rather speedily. Since the first sighting of the gentleman in this grand room, visitors have seen him on at least two more occasions.

On the first floor are the rooms used by William Cavendish as his personal retreat, and it is in his private chamber that women sometimes say that they feel a hand touching them – men, it seems, are ignored.

Ironically enough it is a small, plain room that is perhaps the most haunted in the whole castle. This grey panelled, wooden-floored room overlooks the entrance courtyard and it is believed to have been the room of a housekeeper, possibly a Mrs

A postcard showing the Little Castle in 1905.

BOLSOVER CASTLE

A view of the South Drive, 1915.

Robbins, who lived in the castle during the nineteenth century. For a number of years the castle was home to two successive vicars of Bolsover, with the second incumbent, the Revd John Hamilton Grey, employing a number of staff to cater for his needs and it is thought that he was the one that employed the unfortunate housekeeper, who was to die in this room through illness. Many visitors ask who it is that stands in the corner of this room near to a small doorway that lies diagonally opposite the

Bolsover Castle.

entrance door. All of them give the same description of a diminutive woman dressed in a black and white Victorian dress, many add that they can smell lavender; some say they smell tobacco while others complain of a tightness in the chest and a shortness of breath. On one occasion two members of staff entered the room and although the first staff member was standing just feet away from the second, the latter had effectively disappeared into a white mist, with the first member of staff unable to see her.

In the kitchen the figure of a distressed young woman is seen coming down the stairs, crossing the stone-flagged floor and entering into the bakery, where she furtively tosses a bundle that she has been cradling in her arms into the now long-dead flames. On occasions a cry is heard to come from the package. Perhaps she was trying to cover up some shameful incident by disposing of the unfortunate evidence.

Most of the ghosts at Bolsover are friendly, but some have a mischievous streak, as discovered by a member of staff showing a group of visitors around many years ago. During the tour the guide passed a rather disparaging remark about William Cavendish, which was soon forgotten, however with the tour over and the guests gone, the guide was leaving the Little Castle by the main steps at the front when an unseen hand pushed her down, causing her to hurt her ankle. Looking around she could see that she was totally alone – it was the last time she ever made an unkind remark about her long dead host.

In the walled garden the children of visitors quite often report that they have been joined by another child which the parents are unable to see. When questioned, the children describe their new friend as a boy dressed in an old style of clothing. Who he is no one knows, but he is separate to the figure seen walking around the top of the garden wall on occasions or the soldiers said to march down the main driveway in front of the ruined Terrace range.

thirteen

Sookholme, Lukin and the Monks

When you go through the doorway and enter into Church Warsop's parish church of St Peter and Paul, spare a moment and take a look to your left. On the wall you will see a number of plaques remembering souls who have long since passed away. Behind the door and quite high up on the wall is a wonderful marble tablet placed there in memory of John Rolleston of Sokeholme Hall [*sic*], who was given the estate by William Cavendish after the restoration of the monarchy in 1660 as a gift for helping to protect his lands while he was in exile. There are a number of other plaques close by dedicated to members of the Lukin family, one of which tells us that Henry Lukin of Sokeholme Hall [*sic*] was born in 1586 at Great Badden, Essex, and died in the Hall in 1630. The building accounts of 1613 for Bolsover Castle show that a Lukin from Sookholme provided building materials for its construction, but then, strangely, his name is mentioned no more. Tradition has it that one of the Lukin family took himself to a top floor garret in the Hall and committed suicide there,

Sookholme church, the only religious building left in the village.

Sookholme, where a bird watcher saw a group of ghostly monks.

leaving his spirit in torment. The room itself became known as 'Lukin's garret', which leaves the question, is the Lukin who disappeared from the building accounts the same person who took his own life? Unlike his relatives, the man who committed suicide did not get a plaque placed on the wall of Warsop Church. Perhaps the local populace had him buried on unconsecrated ground near to a crossroads, so that his soul would not know which way to go; in addition to this he would have had a piece of stone covering his eyes so he could not see his way, and a wooden stake driven into his side.

Sookholme's small Norman church stands a short distance back from the main road and close to a side road, amid the fields of the local farms. Imagine the look of shock that must have passed over the face of one birdwatcher late one summer's night in 1925 as he stared in amazement at a procession of twelve hooded and robed figures walking single file along the road, each with his hand on the shoulder of the ghostly form in front. This was certainly a strange vision to behold in such a quiet, out-of-the-way place, especially when the only religious building nearby was the old church which was never home to monks. There was however thought to be a monastery nearby many years ago. The manor had been owned by the Priory of St Oswald at Nostell in Yorkshire, and it is probable that the monks set up some kind of religious house at Sookholme. The only evidence that one ever existed used to be a square of old yew trees that grew near to the road right up to the late nineteenth or early twentieth centuries. A formation of yews like this normally indicates the presence of a religious house close by.

fourteen

Mill Cottage . . .

In the mid-1980s, Peter Harrison and his wife-to-be Carole moved into their idyllic home at the side of the mill in Ollerton village. The picturesque setting was the ideal place for them – with the countryside on their doorstep and work only a short distance away. Over the next two years life settled into its usual pattern, until early one morning. At about 5 a.m. Peter was downstairs making a fire in the lounge grate in order to take the chill out of the room after a cool night, when he heard a creaking from the wooden stairs that led down from the bedroom. Assuming that Carole had got up earlier than normal he carried on in his task, but within a couple of minutes he realised he was still alone. Wondering where Carole was he called out to her, but, when no reply came, he decided to investigate the noise and see precisely where she had gone. As he made his way out of the room he glanced at the back door, only to see the keys swinging in the lock. Further examination showed the door had been unlocked. Peter assumed that his wife had gone outside, yet no one had passed him as he had prepared the fire so he went upstairs to check Carole's whereabouts. She was fast asleep in bed. Had there been an intruder? Definitely not … but who had unlocked the door from the inside? The mystery was never solved.

Soon this curious event passed to the back of the couple's minds and life returned to normal until a little over a year later, when strange things began to happen. At around 1 a.m. one morning Peter was woken from a deep and pleasant sleep by his wife, who claimed she could hear noises coming from somewhere outside the bedroom. As the couple lay there, the sound of chains moving around gears (later described as similar to a block and tackle being used) filled the room, but with the sound fading away the couple drifted off to sleep again. Within minutes though the couple were awake again, the sound of the chains louder than ever. Resolving to get to the bottom of things, Peter put on the light to investigate, only to be taken aback as the noise stopped. Turning off the light made the noise return, while having the light on brought silence. Despite feeling genuinely uneasy, Peter tried to put his wife's mind at rest by explaining that the sound was just the miller next door starting work earlier than usual – an explanation that even he did not believe.

After a restless and uneasy night the couple rose in the morning and made their way to the kitchen, where they found their pet Dachshund cowering in fear in the corner of the room while scattered around were the remnants of the dog's blue plastic bowl; it had eaten the remainder of the bowl. What had caused those strange noises

Mill Cottage and the watermill.

and had scared the dog so remained a mystery. The miller who worked next door had not come to work early that day and the slaughterhouse to the rear of the cottage only worked one day a week, and it was not the day in question. But perhaps the answer to the puzzle lay closer to home than was first thought. The cottage is a converted former rope shop, so is it possible that the sound of the chains is that of a long dead worker returning to finish his days' work, or is it something to do with the soul of the man hanged in the area behind the slaughterhouse and mill, as legend claims?

Whatever the reason, the present owners of Mill Cottage have had no such experience ... so perhaps all is well again.

fifteen

... and The Snooty Fox

Just a short distance from the old mill in Ollerton stands the attractive Snooty Fox pub, a place to sit and watch the world go by while enjoying a cool drink and tasty food, while just a few feet away the river that drives the old mill provides a scenic backdrop. The building in which the pub resides dates back to Georgian times when it was built as a farmhouse – at that time called Forest House – with its conversion into a public house taking place in the twentieth century. During this time it has no doubt seen many events, both happy and sad, take place within its walls. Like all old buildings it seems to talk to you as you wander through the rooms, with creaks and groans coming from all directions as the aged timbers move and flex, yet still, with all this history around you, your eye is drawn to a photograph that sits on the shelf behind the bar.

This photograph appears to be a copy of one taken many years ago and shows an elderly couple who seem to have had a full life and now in their twilight years are comforted in their love for each other. On the back of the photograph in faded writing are a few words, including the name of the lady, Clarissa Leonora Jones, and the dates of her birth and death. It was this photograph that was to prove troublesome for one landlord in particular.

On 30 June 2009 a new landlord arrived to take over the pub and, like all new occupants of a property, he made a few small adjustments here and there so that he felt more at home and happy about how things were set out. Picking up the photograph of Mr and Mrs Jones, the landlord examined it with interest and then, instead of replacing it in its original position, he placed it casually on a drinks chiller. Within a short time the chiller had stopped working and needed to be replaced. Unaware that the problem might be connected to the photograph,

The Snooty Fox with the watermill in the background.

the publican moved the picture onto the cash register; this too broke down and had to be replaced. Once again the resting place of the picture was changed, and the landlord ended up replacing yet another drinks chiller. When the photograph was placed on top of the machine used for washing dirty glasses that too broke down and a workman had to be called in to repair it. Finally, one of the locals advised the landlord to put the picture back in its original position behind the bar. The publican duly obliged and since that day no electrical machinery has failed. But why should a photograph of an elderly couple be the source of so much trouble? Legend has it that Mr and Mrs Jones lived on a plantation at one time, possibly in Africa, and that their lives had been active and their love for each other deep. When Mr Jones died, Clarissa was so broken-hearted that she took herself to the third floor attic of this old building and hanged herself.

Sadly the legend is not true. Clarissa and her husband had been in the hotelier trade since 1906 when they took there first position in Sheffield, eventually finding their way to the Hop Pole Hotel at Ollerton in 1916. The couple ran this establishment for many years and even when her husband sadly died in 1938, Clarissa carried on by herself until 1947, when she decided it was time to step aside. Wishing to be with her family, she simply crossed the road to live with her son and daughter at Forest House, where she died three years later after a long illness at the grand old age of eighty-one. But what about the photograph and the trouble with the electrical equipment? Well, that certainly did happen, so maybe Clarissa just wants visitors to admire the picture and the mischievous old lady plays pranks if it is moved.

But what about the story of the hanging? When a medium took a group around the Snooty Fox they made their way up the stairs to the attic. As one of the visitors looked out of the window, much to her alarm she saw in the reflection an elderly woman hanged by the neck, while two other ladies came down the stairs in a state of distress and left the building immediately. The Snooty Fox is a very old building so it is quite possible that some unrecorded tragedy did take place during its history and the spirit of this poor soul is unable to leave. Clarissa, it seems, is not alone.

The Snooty Fox, which could be haunted by more than one ghost

sixteen

The Philosopher and Hardwick Old Hall

ardwick Hall is one of the country's best known and most admired Elizabethan country houses, attracting tourists from all over the world who come to see its sumptuous interior and beautiful architecture, which has been described as 'more glass than wall'. With the view to the front overlooking the valley below and surrounded by its own parkland, its setting is truly impressive. Imagine what it must have been like all those years ago when, on first sight of the Hall, you began to realise the power, wealth and importance of the woman who was to be your host – Elizabeth, Countess of Shrewsbury, also known as 'Bess of Hardwick'. Building work began on the house in the 1590s to provide Bess with a new house that would reflect her status in the world, while just a few yards away lies the house that was her birthplace and was to be the forerunner to her new home.

The Old Hall, as it became known, still stands in the shadow of the new house but today, unlike the New Hall, is a ruin and only a hint of its former grandeur and glory is visible in the high walls and the remaining ornate and highly decorative plasterwork. This building is much older than its younger neighbour and the fact that it was ever built into the once impressive building that it became is only because of a series of improbable events.

Hardwick Old Hall in the 1930s.

The story of Bess of Hardwick is almost one of rags to riches and it was only through a series of unlikely experiences that led this strong-willed woman to become one of the most powerful women in England. When Bess was born at Hardwick in about 1527, she entered into a more humble household that her family had occupied since at least the thirteenth century. Within a year of Bess's birth her father had died and after a series of financial and personal difficulties for the family, she was married off at the age of fifteen to Robert Barley. Her husband, who was younger than her, died only a year later, leaving Bess and her family with little prospect for the future, yet, as time passed, she met and married William Cavendish, a man twenty-two years her senior. The marriage to this wealthy and influential government official produced eight children in a union that lasted over ten years, before the untimely death of William Cavendish once again brought tragedy. Cavendish had been a Commissioner for the Dissolution of the Monasteries while working for Henry VIII and the new Queen Mary had implicated him in corrupt activities, so it was possibly the stress of the situation that led to his demise. Of the eight children that came from William and Bess's marriage, only six survived infancy.

Bess's third husband was William St Loe, another older man, and his mysterious death, possibly from poison, led to questions about his wife's motives for marriage. Her fourth and final husband was George Talbot, 6th Earl of Shrewsbury. Following their wedding in 1567, they became one of the most powerful couples in the country, with vast estates and property bringing a wealth that most people can only dream of.

Talbot was soon to be made the captor of Mary Queen of Scots and this odious duty soon put a strain on the marriage and, by the late 1570s, it was obvious that the marriage was doomed to failure and so Bess moved back to her beloved family home of Hardwick. In June 1583, Bess bought Hardwick for herself after her brother James, who owned the property, had died heavily in debt. This was the start of a building process that would transform the old place into something more fit for her station

Hardwick New Hall in about 1906; the ruins of the old Hall lay just a few yards away.

in life. The Old Hall, as it was to become known, became a hive of activity with staff and servants thronging the rooms and corridors amid the hustle and bustle of a large country house that was moving with the times.

Even with the Old Hall undergoing a complete makeover Bess still wanted more, so before building works were completed she started the new Hall just a few yards away. This was to be her main home while the Old Hall served its purpose as quarters for her servants and some members of her family. When Bess died in 1608, Hardwick passed to her favourite son, William, who employed Thomas Hobbes, a great philosopher, as tutor to his son, another William. Hobbes was a very learned and travelled man and his thoughts and ideas were at times controversial, leading him into occasional conflict with his peers and the government. As a practical man he used to experiment with early forms of telescopes and indulge himself in the newly-built library in the Old Hall; his mind was thought to be exceptional and far above that of the common man. With all this daily activity and such intense characters walking the corridors of country power, there is no wonder Hardwick Old Hall is considered one of the most haunted places in the county.

Strangely enough it is not the main building that is subject to these spectral visitations but the West Lodge, a building now used as an entrance to the grounds of the Old Hall as well as a shop, exhibition area and offices.

As you enter the lodge you see in front of you a long passageway on the left upon which there are two doors, the first door taking you into the shop while the second leading out of the shop and back into the passage. Just beyond the doors on the left is a set of stairs leading to the upper floors, and next to this is another stairway leading to the grounds of the Hall. At the far end of the passage is a doorway that leads down to the staff area. Enter into the shop and you are met by a small room lined with display cabinets and a sales counter, behind which is a window that looks onto the grassed courtyard. It is this room that has been the scene of many strange and unexplainable happenings.

One long-standing member of staff began work there in mid-1999 and, with the large numbers of visitors constantly passing through the door, she found it both enjoyable and at times stressful tending the shop and site alone. At the end of one particularly hard day, as she was preparing to cash up, she heard a loud thud from the floor to her right. There, lying in front of one of the cabinets, was a book that had dropped off the shelf. Replacing it she got back to work when, once again, there was a thud as the book hit the floor for a second time. Again she replaced it on the shelf. There was no wind or any kind of vibration to cause the book to fall, yet every time she replaced it a short time later it would leap onto the floor. In total she replaced the book four times before politely asking it to stay where it was, and, miraculously, it did. Not wishing to be labelled mad she kept the incident to herself.

But things did not end there. Every morning one of the books that had been on display would be found neatly and precisely placed on the floor of the shop, even though the door had been locked all night and access was not possible. To this very day this still happens.

Then she started to hear footsteps in the room upstairs. When she investigated the noise she found the door closed and the room empty, yet when she returned to the shop downstairs the noise began once more. Each of the doors in the shop is fitted with a special mechanism that allows the door to be opened wide to allow easy access, but in the event of fire they automatically close by means of a strong spring mechanism and once activated the doors will close fully. Time and again our puzzled member of staff heard the exit door from the shop creaking and, when she looked up from her work, would see it partly closed – something that should not have been possible because of the strong spring mechanism – and on one occasion she saw a shimmering shape pass across the doorway and move down the corridor.

Another member of staff watched in disbelief as the screws holding the door handle in place slowly rotated in an anti-clockwise direction, and this same person once saw the figure of a man walking beside the perimeter wall. The description she gave was that of the philosopher Thomas Hobbes, who had expressed the wish to be buried at his beloved Hardwick but was instead interred at Ault Hucknall parish church. It is said he walks the walls trying to get back into the Hall so he can get to his library or own room.

The sound of stones and grit hitting the shop window with extreme force or what was described as the sound of a great wind rattling the windows has been heard even though no wind or breeze has been present and no visitors were on site to play a joke because the site was closed at that time. Keys have gone missing from safe places, only to be found on the grass outside, and the figure of a lady dressed in a flowing blue gown has been seen flitting around the grounds.

Our long-standing member of staff eventually confided in a colleague about the curious incidents she had experienced, only to find out that her companion had also been subject to the same phenomena. In an attempt to find out if they could induce something to happen, they dared the spirits to perform some act to prove that they were there – sadly nothing happened, until they began talking about work and their frustrations came to the surface. As they became more agitated there was the sound of a sudden rushing and whooshing of air from the corridor and the automatic alarms on the fire doors activated, filling the room with noise. Within seconds the noise had stopped and, with a loud whirring noise, the alarms reset themselves, something totally impossible because the battery power supply had to be removed to allow the alarms to reset.

Then it was noticed that the only door that was causing problems was the one that exited the shop and not the entry door. A look at the old plans of the building showed that the exit door was originally the only door in the room and the entry door was a modern addition.

More than one person has heard the sound of children coming from one of the upstairs rooms when no one was there, and it has also been noticed that any ghostly activity ceases if the person experiencing the torment asks for it to stop. Are these events the result of ghostly children playfully teasing members of staff? After all, it is believed that Hobbes used the West Lodge as a schoolroom to teach children and the chastising from an adult might make them settle down. Considering the vast scale of the ruins, it is curious that nearly all the eerie happenings that take place here occur in a small building at the entrance and not in the once impressive Hall – or is it? Remember, the West Lodge is where the living spend a great deal of their time, so perhaps the spirits are roaming the Old Hall out of sight and free to do as they wish.

seventeen

The Carnarvon Arms and the Ship Room

Teversal is an ancient village established long before William the Conqueror won the Battle of Hastings and, at the time of the Domesday Book in 1086, it was large enough to be recorded and known as Tevershalt. Throughout the centuries it has had a number of different names, each one a corruption or variation in spelling of the original. The 'sal' part of one of the later spellings is taken from the Saxon word that translates as 'a seat or dwelling, mansion, palace or hall', which gives an indication that someone of wealth possibly had a building of substance here. Any evidence of such a substantial building from that era has long since gone, but careful observation of the village reveals a surprising history hidden behind a modern frontage.

One of the oldest buildings in the area is the Carnarvon Arms, an ancient coaching inn that is thought to date back about 400 years. Originally known as the Cross Keys, it was ideally placed on the main road near to the junction with the road from Pleasley to pick up the passing trade from wayfarers and coaches alike. It was only in about 1870 that the Cross Keys changed its name and became the Carnarvon Arms, taking its name from the Earls of Carnarvon, who were Lords of the Manor from 1830 to 1929.

The Carnarvon.

Four hundred years of habitation has made this public house a place of interest and strange happenings. Old buildings creak and groan as they settle down but that doesn't account for the sound of footsteps that have been heard upstairs when no one is there, nor does it account for the sound of voices heard in rooms that have been empty. Doors that had been locked have been found swinging open with no explanation as to why, objects placed on shelves were seen to fall – or were knocked off by invisible hands, and lights would be turned on after they had been turned off. Most spookily of all has been the sound of clocks striking thirteen or stopping entirely and becoming silent.

At the side of the main bar is a door that leads into 'The Ship Room', a wonderful room designed by someone with true imagination and flair. As you enter you are met with a vision of the inside of a sailing ship with deep, rich, dark-coloured panelling. At the far end, opposite the entrance door, are a series of large windows set into a wall that slopes outwards at the top, giving the impression of being in the stern of a ship. The whole room is a marvel that dates back to the 1930s, when the Carnarvon Arms was owned by The People's Refreshment and Holiday Association, who decided to have a change around. The Ship Room was originally the private accommodation of the landlord until 1936, when this new room was constructed, giving the Carnarvon a special retreat. It is thought that D.H. Lawrence stayed in Teversal for a short time while he was writing *Lady Chatterley's Lover* and that he wrote part of the book while visiting the Carnarvon. There is no proof of this, but some of the locations mentioned in the book do seem to match those in the area. Lawrence would not have used the Ship Room because his infamous book was written in the 1920s, before the room was built, but if he did visit the Carnarvon he might have used the landlord's rooms for privacy.

In the corner to the left of the false windows is said to sit the ghost of a man drinking out of an old style metal drinking vessel, while opposite him, in the corner to the right of the windows, sits a woman and child, some say a dog, who quietly watches. This corner is also where a cold spot can be felt on occasions. Mediums sometime take parties into this small and intimate function room in an attempt to find out who these characters are, but in reality we may never know. Or will we?

The Ship Room in the Carnarvon, where a ghost is seen sitting in the corner.

eighteen

The Spectres of Sutton Scarsdale Hall

eath, war, squandered fortunes and adulterous affairs are usually confined to the pages of fiction, but visit just about any old ruined house and you can feel that those bare walls are hiding some dark and strange secret that are just waiting to be told.

Standing a little way back from the M1 near Heath sits Sutton Scarsdale Hall, a once fine country house that sat in its own grounds overlooking the Vale of Scarsdale. The present hall is believed to be the fifth house that has stood on this site, and throughout history it has gone through a number of turbulent times. Originally owned by the Saxon Wolfric Spott, the land was left in his will to the monks of Burton Abbey, who forfeited the land after the Norman Conquest. Various owners developed the land over the coming generations but it was the Leake family that are first recorded as definitely living in a house there.

The upwardly mobile Leake family were raised to the peerage in 1624 when Francis Leake was given the title of Lord Deincourt. This ardent Royalist fought on the side of Charles I during the Civil War and after a siege laid down by Parliamentary forces lost Sutton Scarsdale, managing to escape to Newark in an attempt to rejoin the Royalist cause. His efforts did not go unrecognised and he was created 1st Earl of Scarsdale in 1645.

When King Charles was executed, the Earl was so distraught he had a grave dug in St Mary's Church next door and every Friday he would dress in sack cloth and ashes and lay in the open grave deep in thought and prayer. If legend is true then Francis Leake was not the first of his family to make use of the church in a way other than was originally intended. The story goes that many years ago Sir Nicholas Leake left the Hall to join the Crusades. Before he left for the Holy land this brave and courageous knight and his wife broke a ring in half, each vowing to keep their half as a token of their love for each other. Luck was not on Sir Nicholas's side, for after one battle he was captured by the enemy. Many years of incarceration followed, with his resolve starting to fail as time went on, until, in a plea for help, he turned to God and prayed, saying that if he could be returned home so that he could see his beloved wife once again he would provide food for the poor of the parish.

When he woke up from his nights' sleep he was astonished to find himself sitting in the porch of Sutton Scarsdale Church, close to his home, however, when he presented himself at his home, he was refused entry. His appearance had changed and instead of a fine, well-dressed nobleman, here now stood a dishevelled and dirty wretch. Realising

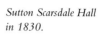

there was only one way to make everyone believe who he was, he reached inside his clothing and pulled out his half of the broken ring, asking for it to be given to his wife. When she saw the ring she knew it really was her husband standing there and that he was not long-dead as she had feared. Years of prosperity followed, but Sir Nicholas did not forget his promise and provided the poor with bread on St Nicholas Day, a tradition that continued until 1736, when the last of the Leakes died.

The last of the Leake family to live in the house was Nicholas Leake, 4th Earl of Scarsdale. In 1724 he set upon an ambitious programme to transform his home into the vast country house, which stands as an empty shell today. Over the next four years he employed the architect Francis Smith of Warwick to make sweeping changes, and the finest of craftsmen were brought to the site. By the time Nicholas Leake died in

Staff at Sutton Scarsdale Hall, c. 1870.

Sutton Scarsdale Hall stable block.

1736, the house had cost him so much money he was in debt to nearly £100,000, and it was this, and other episodes in his life, that many believe led Hogarth to base the 'Rake' in his 'Rake's Progress' on the 4th Earl of Scarsdale.

Once more the house changed ownership until, in 1824, it was acquired by Richard Arkwright, described as the 'richest commoner in England', for his son Robert. In that same year Henry Bramwell is recorded as accidently drowning when he fell backwards into the water trough at the Hall.

The Arkwrights – the last occupants of the Hall – have left behind a legacy that even they would be surprised at, for they and the Hall are possibly the inspiration for D.H. Lawrence's novel *Lady Chatterley's Lover*. Following the First World War, the land around the Hall was sold off but the house itself failed to get a buyer, so it was dismantled and sold off piecemeal, leaving behind an empty shell that still stands today as a reminder of more prosperous times.

When you walk between the high barren walls, remember that you are not alone, as there have been many sightings of ghostly activity. The sound of footsteps are often heard when there is no one in the area and, although the whole site is open to the elements, the smell of tobacco freely pervades the air at times. Disembodied body parts are seen floating through the atmosphere, while walkers who take the path that runs around the Hall have seen strange floating lights moving among the ruins.

Early one morning during the late 1960s, a man and his son witnessed a white hooded, legless phantom that glided effortlessly in the churchyard beside the Hall. This ghostly spirit, with slits for eyes, made its way through the gravestones while emitting the sound of sobbing or crying.

The empty shell of Sutton Scarsdale Hall.

During the 1970s another man and his son were walking up the main driveway away from the house, but when they turned and looked back at the Hall they were horrified to see a woman tearfully waving in their direction from a window on the upper floor. The two spectators turned and fled as they realised that the shape they could see was hovering in the air, since all the floors and ceilings had long ago been removed.

One of the most spooky parts of the house lies underground in the vaults and cellars that still exist. The only way into this subterranean complex is down a set of stone steps that are sealed off by a locked iron gate – a wise precaution. A hand is seen to hover at the entrance to the steps, seemingly beckoning those who see it to enter and make their way down below ground level to meet their doom. In this dark, dank setting many unusual things have taken place. Dark shapes that take human form have been seen flitting in and out of the shadows and once again unexplained footsteps have been heard. There are claimed to be tunnels running from the cellars to the nearby woods and that some dark deed took place in one of them. Is this why the figure of a monk has been seen in the nearby woodland? After all, the land was once owned by the monks of Burton Abbey – was an evil act committed on one of those men of religion?

nineteen

The Fox and Hounds and the Friendly Ghost

From a young age children are taught the romantic fable of Robin Hood and his merry men and how they robbed the rich to give to the poor. They learn of the jolly Friar Tuck and the strong Little John, who stood side-by-side with Robin and the rest of the band of outlaws to fight the villainous Sherriff of Nottingham. Local children might even be told how Maid Marion was born at Cuckney and that she married Robin in Edwinstowe, only to lose her love at the hands of the Prioress at Kirklees Abbey. Blidworth is also part of the legend, for it is said that Will Scarlet lies buried within the village churchyard. Perhaps this is fantasy and then again perhaps it is not, for many folk legends have their basis in truth.

Just outside the village stands a strange looking stone that rises over 14ft high and has a large, curious hole through the centre. This naturally-occurring stone is known as the Druid Stone and was supposedly used by Druids for religious purposes because the hole in the far side faces the midsummer sunrise. A more probable use for this strange outcrop of rock was as a place for women to take their children so they could gain protection from rickets. The children would be passed through the central hole and thus be spared the horrors of this terrible disease. Once again there is no proof that the stone was ever used for this purpose, however it stands close to Ricket Lane and so that could be the clue to its real use.

Some years ago a man out walking his dog stopped near the stone for a quick rest. As he stood there he noticed an eerie silence fall around him, and his dog became agitated, staring and growling in the direction of the Druid Stone. Taking fright, the man left quickly with his dog but as they made their way from the field, the dog kept turning to look back at the stone, growling menacingly. It was not until they were some distance away that the dog finally settled down.

Not all ghosts and spirits make themselves known to human beings, and even if they do, there is nothing to say that they will create such a fuss that it is obvious they are there. Very often the ghost is quiet and goes about its business without arousing the suspicion of those nearby – unless it is seen or felt by someone who just happens to be in the right place at the right time. One such ghost regularly makes itself felt at the Fox and Hounds pub at Blidworth Bottoms. This welcoming pub is part of a small hamlet

The Druid Stone Blidworth.

that sits a short distance from Blidworth itself and is surrounded by open fields and nearby forests

Nowadays Blidworth Bottoms is made up of just a few houses, farm buildings and stable yards, with the Fox and Hounds providing a place of refreshment and entertainment, but many years ago the whole area was much more vibrant and industrial. Apart from cottages for the local workers and labourers there were shops and a post office to supply the needs of the locals, while some of the cottages were used by framework knitters who toiled long hours trying to make a living. One of the shops that plied its trade may have had a double life as a nail makers and the original location of the Fox and Hounds. At some point the licence transferred to the present building, which was erected during the early part of the nineteenth century as a farmhouse. The exact date of the changeover is unknown, however the present Fox and Hounds has been here for a very long time.

The ghost that resides at the Fox and Hounds is not the sort of spirit that throws objects around or makes threatening noises; nonetheless you will still be aware that it is there. You may get the sensation that someone is watching you, or you might catch a fleeting glimpse of a moving shape out of the corner of your eye. Objects will mysteriously move from one place only to be found in another.

Just once the ghost might have come out of hiding to show itself to a member of staff. When all the customers had gone home late one Sunday night a female member

The Fox and Hounds, Blidworth Bottoms. (David and Diane Cole)

The bar inside the Fox and Hounds. (David and Diane Cole)

of staff was alone in the bar area, the entire kitchen staff were busily cleaning up after a hectic evening's work and she was alone – or so she thought. Her attention was drawn to the bar where she saw a large man, whom she described as wearing a white shirt. Momentarily glancing away and then returning her gaze to the bar, she was startled to see that the man had completely vanished. He could not have left the pub by any of the doors because they were all locked and he had not gone into any of the other rooms nor had he passed through the kitchen. It was as if he had never existed. The identity of the ghost is far from clear and his name will probably never be known, but the question still remains – did the ghost leave the bar by using the secret, sealed-off spiral staircase, and is this the same spirit that makes the Fox and Hounds such a welcoming place?

twenty

Rufford Abbey and the Death's Head Monk

Close to the heart of Sherwood Forest lies Rufford Abbey, a once grand and magnificent country house that fell into decline and partial ruin. Walking around the country park, the remains of the abbey and its complex of outbuildings gives only a hint to the once glorious house that used to attract royalty and high society to parties and balls here.

The story of Rufford Abbey began in the twelfth century, when monks from Rievaulx Abbey in North Yorkshire travelled to the area to make a 'daughter house' on land that they had been given by Gilbert the Earl of Lincoln. The monastery prospered and grew over the years until the Black Death ravaged the country and, slowly but surely, Rufford went into a gradual decline. There is little doubt that in the beginning the majority of the monks were pious and God-fearing men who followed their beliefs with a diligence that can only be admired, however standards and the moral behaviour among the monks inside the abbey had at times been dubious, with the Christian beliefs of a few of the monks open to question. In the thirteen century Brother William was arrested for the murder of another Brother, while in the early fourteenth century two of the monks joined with some locals to rob and kidnap Thomas de Holme. Later that century, when the abbey was inspected, the two inspectors found that the behaviour of the monks was well below standard, and that they enjoyed pursuits that were not of the religious and pious kind. They also noticed that the monks had taken to not wearing the habits of the office as required and instead were wearing more fashionable, and presumably more comfortable, clothes. To try and remedy this lack of discipline in the abbey, a strict set of rules were implemented.

The final death knell for the abbey came when Henry VIII broke with the Church of Rome and closed many religious houses, including Rufford Abbey. In 1537 the abbey was granted to George Talbot, the 4th Earl of Shrewsbury, but it wasn't until the 6th Earl of Shrewsbury, another George, took over that Rufford's fortunes began to change. A long process of building and royal patronage started, heralding a new dawn in Rufford Abbey's history and standing.

For generations the abbey became the home of successive families of aristocrats, each leaving their own mark on the land and buildings. In 1939 the Army took over

The entrance to Lime Tree Avenue, Rufford Abbey.

the house and its grounds. By 1952 the abbey was in the hands of Nottinghamshire County Council and just four years later a slow process of demolition began in order to save the remaining sound parts of the structure.

With such a long and varied past it is no surprise that stories of ghosts and hauntings in the old abbey and its grounds have been told for many years, even when it was a family home.

Female guests who visited the house in its heyday would claim that they had been woken in the night by a baby or young child nestling up to them for comfort, while in reality no child was in the house. This poor child was described as being frightened, crying, feeling cold and shivering. Who the child is no one will ever know, but legend has it the child was murdered in one of the abbey's bedrooms. While the identity of this sad child will forever be a mystery, the identity of the White Lady might be known. This shadowy white figure, seen gliding around the gardens and ruins of the abbey on its endless quest, is said to be the ghost of Lady Arbella Stuart, the granddaughter to Bess of Hardwick. Bess had arranged the hurried and secret marriage of her daughter, Elizabeth, to Charles Stuart, brother of Mary Queen of Scots. The product of this union was Arbella, who, in later years, was seen by James I as a threat to the throne, particularly after her secret marriage and elopement to William Seymour. After her recapture, James had her imprisoned in the Tower of London, where she eventually died at aged just forty. Arbella it is said has returned to one of the places of her

An omen of what lies inside? A face on the gate post of Rufford Abbey.

childhood, where she had so much fun and enjoyment, far away from the troubles of the royal court.

Should you see the White Lady you are fortunate indeed, but beware the Black Friar. If you see this fearsome spectre it could be the portent of bad things to come. The Black Friar will make his way towards his unsuspecting victims, while all the time keeping his face hidden by keeping his head bowed down as he draws close, until, finally, he raises his head to expose not a face but a skull – the Death's Head. Many years ago one poor man who witnessed the full fury of the Black Friar was so distressed by what he saw that he died shortly afterwards. The parish records even have an entry recalling the incident, with the words 'died from fright after seeing the Rufford ghost'. Just a few years ago a group of four men were in the grounds of the abbey one cold winter's day when, in the ground-hugging mist, they saw a black shape moving slowly. As they watched, they saw the shape glide in front of the ruins and down the steps towards the undercroft. Strangely, though, the monks of Rufford Abbey wore white or brown habits, not black, so is the Black Friar a visitor who never left?

With all these ghostly apparitions, don't be surprised if one more should suddenly appear in front of you. The sight of an elderly lady pushing a pram in the park is not uncommon, however this particular woman is dressed in Victorian-style clothing and pushes an old-fashioned perambulator around. Should you decide to approach her she will ignore you and simply go on her own way, until at last she disappears.

twenty-one

The Duke and the Quiet Spirit

At the bottom of a series of twisting stone steps that are reached from behind the public bar, you enter the cellar of the Duke of Wellington, reputedly the oldest public house in Kirkby in Ashfield. This small white-painted room is where, many years ago, a tunnel used to give secret passage to anyone who was able to take advantage of its use. Long since bricked-up, and with the location of the entrance lost many years ago, it has been a source of curiosity for those with knowledge of its existence for decades, but who built this tunnel and, more importantly, why?

The Duke of Wellington.

The nearby church.

The Duke of Wellington has been a public house since the seventeenth century, at that time bearing the name the Silent Lady, yet the original use of the building could have been religious, possibly some kind of church hall or chapel. In 1717, the local rectory was built and with it the tunnel that used to emerge in the cellar of the Silent Lady. It is believed that this passageway once linked the two buildings together, allowing free movement for those inclined to use it. Perhaps the local clergy liked to have a little tipple while appearing to abstain from alcohol? Many years later the Silent Lady was renamed the Duke of Wellington in recognition of the great General and army commander, whose glittering military career culminated in the defeat of Napoleon at the Battle of Waterloo. This accomplished man then became a politician, working his way through the political ranks to become Prime Minister.

Although the Duke of Wellington never visited this public house, over the centuries thousands of local men, women and children have, and it would appear that at least one of them has decided to stay on on a permanent basis. Many a landlord and landlady has experienced strange goings on both downstairs in the bar area, upstairs in the office and in the cellar below. Beer lines have had the gas turned off even when the pub has been open, while at night time any pets would become restless and unable to settle. The oldest part of the pub is the bar area and in here tables and chairs would be discovered in the morning either overturned or stacked up in the middle of the floor, but no noise or disturbance was ever heard alerting the publican of any unusual activity. Upstairs in the office the smell of tobacco would sometimes pervade the air.

The church near the Duke of Wellington with the old rectory behind.

It would be interesting to find out who it is that still resides at the Duke of Wellington; is it a customer from long ago or is it the former user of the passage disagreeing about the revelry and drinking that takes place in the bar? Whoever he (or she) is, they have been resident here for a very long time.

twenty-two

Pleasley Mill and the Wandering Soul

It would stand to reason that the older a place is the more likely it is to be haunted, you might even go as far as to say that the more people that lived or worked in that same place, the greater the chance of some kind of unearthly visitations. Pleasley Vale Mill is one of those old, hidden away factories where life revolved around work, sleep, more work and sometimes death. The first mill was built in 1784 beside the River Meden in a small but deep-sided valley whose road twisted its way through the open countryside towards Mansfield Woodhouse. A number of businessmen clubbed together and bought the site at Pleasley Forge to build a cotton-spinning mill using mechanisation. Over the coming years the mill prospered under the tutelage of the Hollins family, even surviving two disastrous fires that ravaged the mills in the 1850s. For a time the company had to impose huge job losses onto its workforce and the

Pleasley Vale mill in its heyday. (V. and M. Gamble)

Pleasley Mill today.

resultant loss of income must have caused extreme hardship amongst some of the families that relied on the mill for employment, especially those that had more than one family member working there.

Many of the workers were young children, some as young as five, who had been taken from the local workhouses and sent to the mills to provide cheap labour. The work in the mills was hard and dangerous and the mortality rate amongst the children in some of these establishments was appallingly high. The later members of the Hollins family seem to have shown a certain degree of compassion for the children from the workhouses by providing some kind of formal education, something that was required by law but frequently ignored by a large number of mill owners. The Hollins family were by no means perfect and they did stray from what might be seen as the path of good on many occasions. Henry Hollins tried to reduce the wages of a number of children for what might have been seen as false reasoning, and his reputation as a hard slave driver seems to be pretty close to the truth. Like most of the mill owners of the day he made the children work long and arduous hours with little time for rest, and the appalling injuries they suffered crippled and killed many.

It was not until Henry Hollins lost his fight about low wages to one particular family that he decided to step aside and let a more progressive member of his family take over the day-to-day running of the mill.

Pleasley Vale Mill finally closed its doors in 1987 after more than 200 years of production on a site that has had human activity nearby for possibly thousands of years. A cave was discovered close to the mill containing rhinoceros and Mammoth bones indicating that prehistoric men and women had inhabited the cave, possibly nomadic people making use of the shelter it provided. Is it possible that these long-gone ancestors are still here and join more modern-day spirits in haunting the old mill?

With the old site declared a conservation area and industry moving back in, the ghosts and restless spirits of the dead started to make themselves known.

The sounds of machinery, unexplained cries from afar and strange grunting noises have been heard filtering through the corridors and rooms of the mill. If this was the only evidence of phantom-like happenings at the mill then it could soon be dismissed as the creaks and groans of an old building, but it isn't. A building does not make the sound of voices in the corridors, nor can it create lights and shadows in the offices. On the first floor of Mill 1 it is not uncommon for some of those working there to have the sensation of unhappiness come upon them to such a degree it is almost like a depression. Tradition has it that it was on this floor that a woman was raped and killed, and that she periodically makes herself visible on the top floor before, as some say, she takes her own life. The lower halves of bodies have also been witnessed as they walk along through the floors, as if going about their business before the floor level has been altered.

Men, it would appear, become overwhelmed by the sensation of intimidation, believed to be brought on by the spirit of a cruel and dominating overseer from the days of the cotton mill. In one of the reception rooms a woman dressed in black walks

The haunted mill No 1.

An early picture of the mill. (V. and M. Gamble)

Pleasley Mill house. (V. and M. Gamble)

obliviously past other occupants and through the wall, while the ghostly shape of a man is observed to walk from the dye house and into Mill 2 – possibly the same man that is seen inside the dye house itself.

Not all the ghosts are confined to the buildings and some of the more remarkable ones have been seen outside in the forecourt area and in the nearby woods. Children's voices have echoed through the trees when no living beings have been nearby and strange sounds have come from the area where the cotton was transported. More surprisingly, visitors and workers alike have caught site of prehistoric phantoms in the area of the rediscovered cave on many occasions.

These strange tales of ghosts and spectres around the mill pale into insignificance with the story of the man who is seen by night-time delivery drivers to Pleasley Vale. The drivers pull up outside the mill buildings to make their deliveries and, seeing a man standing nearby, they make their way over to him to ask for directions. This solid-looking man ignores the drivers as if they do not exist, which to him they don't. Being ignored, the drivers leave the man alone, bewildered as to why he will not speak. His apparent rudeness has led many of the drivers to complain to security guards and other workers about his behaviour, only to be told that they have just been speaking to the ghost, who is known to make frequent visits.

There may come a time when you decide to visit the Vale and see for yourself the place where these ghosts walk, but if you take your car, then beware. As you drive away, keep a close eye on your rear-view mirror and do not be alarmed if you should see a ghostly figure watching you, but do not turn to look back for there will be no one there.

twenty-three

A Miscellany of Miner Visitations

Tales of phantoms, ghosts and unearthly guests come from every quarter, from open countryside to ancient buildings, as well as more modern ones. The age of a property is no guarantee that it will be haunted, nor the fact that a death took place there. Many sightings of ghosts occur in some of the most unusual and unexpected of places, even hundreds or thousands of feet underground.

Coal mines have always been dangerous places to work and in the past the darkness in some parts of the workings have at times led to some men becoming disorientated and panic-stricken. This is especially true of any novice worker that strayed into an older part of the mine, and it was not unknown for colleagues to be sent out in search of the lost miner.

At Warsop Main Colliery one evening a chock fitter was sent to work in a particular part of the mine, however, when his supervisor tried to contact him later by telephone and tannoy, they found they were unable to reach him. Thus a workmate was sent to check that everything was alright. When the 'missing' miner was found, he was still in the place he had been sent to but was cowering on top of a pile of debris. Bleeding and shaken, he explained how he had seen an extremely bright light coming towards him out of the darkness, which gave way to the face of a man. At this point he turned and fled in panic. Taken back to the surface he retold his story, and a picture of the face he had seen was put on the canteen noticeboard. Not long afterwards, a visiting miner asked about the picture and pointed out that it was a portrait of his brother, who had died in an accident ten years earlier.

This is not the only sighting of ghostly miners at Warsop. It was not uncommon to hear miners returning to the surface and telling stories of being passed by a group of two or three other workers who went right by them without stopping. Many of the witnesses knew that they had seen ghosts simply because no one else was working in that area.

Warsop Main is not alone in having supernatural visitors underground, for there are a number of credible sightings from other local collieries. In 1958 two miners at Shirebrook, independently of each other, saw the eerily glowing shape of Wilfred Hales, a former miner who had died three years earlier. Almost thirty years later, two miners at Clipstone Colliery came across an old-time miner wearing clothing from the 1930s. It was not until the figure put its hand onto the shoulder of one of the miners that the two colleagues took fright and fled as fast as they could.

The headstocks of the former Clipstone colliery

None of the ghosts that have been seen at Warsop, Shirebrook or Clipstone gave the impression of wanting to cause harm or distress to those who saw them, and, if anything, were quite friendly. Such was the case with a man at Silverhill Colliery in the late 1970s as he was travelling alone underground. As he was making his way along he noticed a cap lamp in the distance, yet no matter how fast or slow he walked it was always just ahead of him. Later on he was helping saw some planks when, to his great surprise, his job became much easier, as though someone was holding the saw at the other end and was pushing and pulling in time with him. This sudden and unexpected help gave him such a shock that he had to let go of the handle and, to his utter amazement, he watched as the saw completed another two strokes completely unaided.

twenty-four

... and finally

When the writer L. Lindley penned his *History of Sutton-in-Ashfield* in 1907 he recalls a ghost tale that took place many years ago close to the heart of the busy town centre, a story that needs to be told once more.

At one time there used to be a public right of way called Wood Street that joined together Parliament Street and High Pavement, an access way that a certain 'Mr Jones' would use to get home each time he had been out for a nights entertainment. More times than not Mr Jones would enjoy indulging himself so much that he needed all his wits to find his rather unsteady way home. One evening a friend of Mr Jones decided to play a joke on this poor unfortunate and, taking a white cloth, 'Mr Smith' made his way to the thoroughfare. Donning the garb so that he was completely covered, he stood in the shadows and waited for his friend. Unfortunately for Mr Smith, his victim walked straight past without seeing his ghostly form standing there, so he chased after his friend and began to push against Mr Jones in an attempt to startle him.

To Mr Smith's utter astonishment though, instead of turning and fleeing in fright, Mr Jones turned to the late-night spectre and shouted out, 'Oh, if thou'rt a jostling ghost, here's at the' !', whereupon he then gave the 'ghost' a resounding whack on the head with his walking stick. Mr Smith fled the scene with all due haste and never repeated his joke again.

So, tell me ... after all you have read, do ghosts exist?

Select Bibliography

Books

Anthony, Wayne. *Haunted Nottingham: Myths, Magic and Folklore* (Breedon Books, 2008)

Jacks, Leonard. *The Great Houses of Nottinghamshire and the County Families* (1881)

Lilley, Steve., Fearn, Nathan., and Felix, Richard. *The Ghost Tour of Great Britain: Nottinghamshire* (Breedon Books, Derby, 2006)

Mattews, Robert. *Haunted Places of Nottinghamshire* (Countryside Books, Newbury, 2005)

Moakes, Len. *Haunted Nottinghamshire Volume 2* (J.H. Hall & Sons, Derby, 1993)

Ottewell, David. *Old Ollerton.* (Stenlake Publishing, Catrine, 2002)

Peters, Jane. *Ghosts around Sutton* (North Trent Publishing, 1995)

Smith, Roly. *Rufford Past and Present* (Nottinghamshire County Council, 2000)

Staton, Catherine. *A Ghostly Guide to Nottinghamshire* (Walk and Write.Longcliffe, 2004)

Walkerkine, H. and Buxton, A.S. *Old Churches of Mansfield Deanery* (1907)

Worsley, Lucy. *Hardwick Old Hall* (English Heritage, 1998)

Wright, Gordon and Curtis, Brian J. *The Inns and Pubs of Nottinghamshire* (Nottinghamshire County Council leisure Services, Nottingham, 1995)

Other Sources

www.dmm-pitwork.org

Mansfield Reporter and Sutton-in-Ashfield Times

Oakleaves Magazine

Pall Mall Magazine, 14 (1898)

www.paranormaldatabase.com

St Mary's Church Sutton Scarsdale: A Short History and Guide

White's Directory

Other titles published by The History Press

Haunted Chesterfield
CAROL BRINDLE

Carol Brindle is a Chesterfield Blue Badge Guide and has been conducting historical and ghost walks in the town for a number of years. This collection of stories of apparitions, manifestations, strange sightings and happenings in Chesterfield's streets, churches and buildings will delight those interested in the both the paranormal and darker historical side of the city.

978 0 7524 4081 1

Haunted Peak District
JILL ARMITAGE

This chilling collection of true-life tales details many terrifying accounts of spectres and apparitions which have been documented over the years in the Peak District. Ranging from private residences and graveyards to public houses, tourist attractions, theatres and museums, this book includes many pulse-raising narratives that are guaranteed to make your blood run cold.

978 0 7524 51220

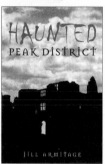

Haunted Derbyshire
JILL ARMITAGE

Drawing on historical and contemporary sources and containing many tales which have never before been published, *Haunted Derbyshire* unearths a chilling range of supernatural phenomena from poltergeists to Victorian spirits. Illustrated with more than fifty archive photographs, this book will delight everyone with an interest in the supernatural history of the area.

978 0 7524 4886 2

Haunted Nottingham
ANDREW JAMES WRIGHT

The streets and buildings of Nottingham are teeming with ghosts, ghouls and things that go bump in the night. *Haunted Nottingham* explores the supernatural side of the city and its surrounding areas and finds many reports of unexplained happenings, weird goings-on and ghostly appearances. The author, Andrew James Wright, has been a ghost investigator for thirty years and has accumulated a vast collection of spooky stories from across the city.

978 0 7524 4194 8

Visit our website and discover thousands of other History Press books.

www.thehistorypress.co.uk

The History Press